CLASSIC EARRING DESIGNS

Written and Illustrated by

Nola May

Eagle's View Publishing Company
6756 North Fork Road
Liberty, UT 84310

ISBN: 0-943604-43-5
Library of Congress Catalog Card Number: 94-70725

FIRST EDITION

10 9 8 7 6 5 4 3 2 1

TABLE OF CONTENTS

ACKNOWLEDGEMENTS

I would like to thank my family and friends for their love and support during my years of beading.

Special thanks to my students, without whom I would never have put together a pattern book.

To all the teachers and Marcie at the Shepherdess, a special thank you. Thank you for all the knowledge you have shared.

Thank you Viola, of Creative Handcrafts, for my first teaching opportunities.

Thank you Kim and Larry of the Indian Store, for the opportunity of teaching classes and helping to keep the craft of beadwork alive and ever growing.

Special thanks to Monte Smith of Eagle's View and Denise, my editor, for hours of work and planning to make this book a reality.

ABOUT THE AUTHOR

Nola May has been designing and experimenting with jewelry and crafts since she was very young. The flowers, plants, orchards and greenhouses of the Wisconsin countryside, which she experienced as a child, have provided her with life-long inspiration for her designs. Her beading became serious when her family moved to New Mexico and she began making jewelry to compliment her wardrobe. This rapidly progressed to taking orders and exhibiting her designs at craft shows. For many years she has collected antique beads and jewelry, researching their era and place of origin. She currently lives in California and teaches classes for craft stores and friends.

INTRODUCTION

This pattern book came about because my students always requested designs. I found myself making individual sketches over and over again. I finally decided to put together a group of different patterns in a book. Some of the patterns are easy and go together quickly. Other patterns will take more time to complete and may be a challenge. There are a variety of techniques in this pattern book; try them all. It is my hope that you will find the instructions and illustrations easy to follow.

I encourage you to change colors and experiment with different bead sizes and types. Being creative can be very rewarding. In designing and choosing color combinations, I have found flowers to be an inspiration. Living in the country, I go for walks and am always filled with new ideas after viewing flowers along the way. Look closely at a flower and you will be amazed and inspired by the blending of colors. Mother Nature will always give you creative ideas.

My wish for you is that you become a great bead designer. I hope this book will be a great help along the path of beading.

MATERIALS NEEDED FOR BEADING

Size #13 English Beading Needles
Nymo Beading Thread - Use size "A" or "O" in white. Nymo also comes in black and other colors.

Beeswax - Wax the thread lightly before working with it to prevent the thread from tangling and fraying.

Scissors - Use the small "stork-shaped" scissors found in fabric and bead stores; these are often used for embroidery and can cut close to the beadwork.

Needle-Nosed Pliers - The kind made specifically for jewelers are best. Use them to attach the ear wires to the loop of the beaded earring.

French Ear Wires - These have a large loop which is opened partway with jewelers pliers and hooked through the beaded earring loop. Then close the ear wire loop with the jewelers pliers.

Clear Fingernail Polish - Applied to the back side of the top of an earring to stiffen it. Do not apply polish to the loop or to the fringe.

Seed Beads - Purchase a variety of colors and sizes; always buy more beads than it seems will be needed. Sizes 9/°, 10/°, and 11/° are used most frequently in these patterns. When buying, look for beads which are uniform in size and shape. SL in pattern legends indicates silver-lined beads.

Bugle Beads - Available in a variety of colors and sizes. Size 11/° seed beads work best with size #2 bugle beads. Size 9/° and 10/° seed beads work best with size #3 or #5 bugle beads. For fringe, use #5 or longer (20mm to 35mm) bugle beads.

Fringe Beads - There are many different beads, available in a variety of sizes and shapes, which add color, texture and weight to an earring when used in the fringe. Experimenting with these can be great fun. Here are some suggestions: Austrian crystals in 4mm and 6mm sizes; Facetted beads (glass or plastic) in 4mm or larger sizes. The fire polish (FP in pattern legends) style made in Czechoslovakia are especially beautiful; Round Druk beads in clear and opaque colors; Tube Satina beads (glass cylinders) in sizes 10x4 and 6x4; Rondells or Spacer beads, in 4mm or 6mm sizes; Crow, Pony, French, Squash, Melon or Rosebud beads; Fetishes made from Mother-of-Pearl or Abalone and carved into shapes such as birds, bears and fish. All of these make great accents in fringe.

GENERAL INSTRUCTIONS

Instructions for creating specific earring styles are given in each chapter. These directions are general in nature and apply when beading any earring design.

Work at a large table with a light shining down on the project. Use about 1 1/2 yards of beading thread, cut at an angle for easy threading through the needle. Wax the thread lightly with beeswax. Use a single thread to bead and **do not** knot the ends of the thread. It is usually not necessary to knot the ends of the thread when the earring is done either; simply weave the thread ends back and forth through the beads in the top of the earring, come down through the base row, and clip off any excess.

It is very important to pick uniform beads (in size and shape) to make the top of an earring. When using bugle beads, it is also important to watch for sharp edges. Do not use these beads, as the edges may cut the thread.

Nymo is a multi-filament nylon thread which stretches when pulled. Use gentle weaving motions rather than tugging or jerking movements when tightening the thread or pulling beads together. If the thread is stretched too much, when it shrinks back to its original shape it will warp the earring body or the fringe. Always be aware of the tension on the thread while beading; keep the beadwork snug, neither too tight nor too loose. Maintaining proper tension gets easier with a little experience.

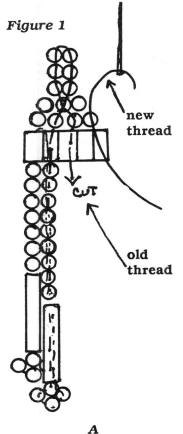

Figure 1

new thread

old thread

A

Most patterns will require two or three lengths of thread (each 1 1/2 yards long) to complete each earring. When six to eight inches of thread remain, it is time to add more thread. To do this, first weave the remaining thread up into the top of the earring; then bring it down through the base row (Figure 1A); choose an area with the fringe already added, if possible. Always leave a tail of the old thread hanging so that it can be pulled back down, should the needle pass through that same base bead(s) again and begin to pop the thread up above the base row. For some reason, if the thread is cut above the base row it shows more than if it is cut below the base row. To secure the new thread, go up through one of the base beads(see Figure 1A), weave through the top

3

beads of the earring, then resume beading where the old thread ran out. When the earring is completed, all the tails of thread should be carefully cut off at the bottom of the base row. Be careful not to cut the threads of the fringe row.

Adding thread provides a good opportunity to reinforce the top loop (see Figure 1A). This loop should always be reinforced at least three times before finishing an earring as it must support the entire weight of the earring.

Sometimes it is necessary to back up and correct a mistake. It is very important to take the needle off the thread before attempting this. Even though it means threading the needle again, this must be done, as the needle can split the thread, resulting in tangles or knots which will slow down the work and may even ruin the piece. For the same reasons, whenever the thread becomes, cut off the frayed portion and re-thread if needed.

When the fringe is completed, weave the thread up into the top of the earring, then down through the base row. If the top of the earring seems too bendable, reinforce it by weaving the thread through more (or all) of the top beads before coming down through the base row. Then cut off all threads that are showing. A thin coat of clear fingernail polish, on the back of the earring top will also stiffen the earring. Do not put nail polish on any of the fringe or top loop beads.

The final step is to add the earwire to the top loop of the earring. Open the attachment loop on the earring with a pair of needle-nosed pliers. Slip the earring loop through the opening, then close the earwire loop with the pliers.

4

COMANCHE WEAVE INSTRUCTIONS

BUGLE BEAD BASE ROWS

The bugle bead base is the most common base row used in the Comanche Weave (also known as the Brick or Comanche Stitch) and it is the easiest to learn.

Begin with 1 1/2 yards of lightly waxed Nymo beading thread on a size #13 beading needle. Put two bugle beads on the thread, sliding them down to about 6 inches from the end (Figure 2A). Leave the tail end of the thread hanging down and put the two bugle beads together, side-by-side (Figure 2B). Go up through the first bugle bead with the needle and thread (Figure 2C), then go back down through the second bugle bead (Figure 2D).

Add a third bugle bead to the thread (Figure 2E). Take the needle down through the top of the second bugle bead (Figures 2F & 2G) and go back up through the third bugle bead (Figure 2H).

Figure 2 (Part I)

A   B   C   D   E   F   G

H   I   J   K

To add a fourth bead to the base row, place it on the thread (Figure 2I), go up through the third bugle bead (Figure 2J) and down through the top of the fourth bugle bead (Figure 2K).

Put the fifth bugle bead on the thread (Figure 2L), go down through the top of the fourth bugle bead (Figure 2M) and then up through the fifth bugle bead (Figure 2N). By repeating this alternate weaving procedure with each new bead, the base row can be made as long as desired.

When all the beads have been added to the base row, weave the needle back through the row of bugle beads (down through the fourth bead, up through the third bead, etc.) End with the thread coming out of the top of the first bugle bead (Figure 2O).

Figure 2 (Part II)

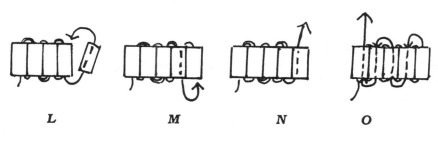

| L | M | N | O |

SEED BEADS TOPS

After the base row is completed, the top of the earring is beaded. Start with the needle and thread coming out of the top of the first bugle (or other base) bead. This first bead should be on the left of the base row and the beginning "tail" thread should hang below it. In this position the front of the earring will face towards the beadworker.

Add one seed bead to the thread. From behind the base row, put the needle under the threads between the first and second base bugle beads (Figure 3A). Pull the needle through, coming out on the front side of the earring. Go back up through the seed bead, making sure to stay in front of the threads between the first two base beads (Figure 3B). The seed bead will be on top of the bugle beads with the hole side up, just like the bugle beads in the base row have their hole sides up. There will

6

be a thread showing to the left of this seed bead (the first in the row).

Put a second seed bead on the thread. Go under the thread between the second and third base bugle beads, then back up through the second seed bead (Figure 3C). In the same manner, add a third seed bead between the third and fourth base bugle beads (Figure 3D) and a fourth seed bead between the fourth and fifth base bugle beads (Figure 3E). There will always be one less bead in this row than there are in the base row.

Turn the earring over so that the tail thread is on the right. This allows the second row of the top to be woven from left to right. Put a new seed bead on the thread. Go under the thread between the first and second seed beads in the first row. Come from the back of the beadwork towards the front. Go back up through the new seed bead (Figure 3F). Continue adding seed beads across the row, using the same technique (Figure 3G). Again, there will be one less bead in this row than in the previous row (Figure 3H).

Figure 3 (Part I)

A   B   C   D

E   F   G   H

7

Turn the earring over again (tail thread on the left) and add the third row of seed beads in the same manner as before (Figure 3I). If a longer base row is used, continue turning the earring over and adding new rows until a two seed bead row has been completed.

Add four seed beads to the thread for the earring loop (Figure 3J). Go down through the left bead in the top row and up through the right bead in the top row. Go through the four beads in the earring loop again and come down through the beads on the left side of the earring top. Continue down through the left hand bugle bead in the base row. The earring is now ready to add the fringe.

Figure 3 (Part II)

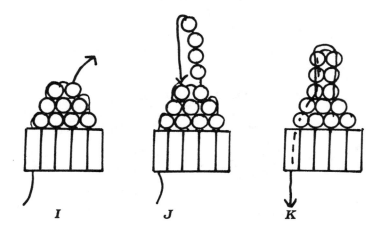

I   J   K

HIDING THE EDGE THREAD

Once the basics of adding beads above the base row to form the earring top are mastered, it will be easy to learn how to hide the thread which shows on the edges of the bead rows. To do this, the first two beads of each row are added at the same time, using the following technique.

At the beginning of each row, put two seed beads on the thread. Go under the thread between the second and third base bugle beads, from back to front, skipping the thread between the first and second base bugle beads (Figure 4A). Go up through the second seed bead (Figure 4B), then down through the first

8

seed bead. Come back up through the second seed bead (Figure 4C). From here, add one seed bead at a time to finish the row. Remember that only the first two beads of each row are woven in this manner.

When using bugle beads in the earring top, this method will be necessary because of the length of thread which is otherwise exposed (not only is this unsightly, but this much exposed thread is very vulnerable to cutting or fraying). Also, when dark beads are used the thread is more visible and should be hidden in the manner described above. Experienced beaders do not leave obvious thread showing.

Figure 4

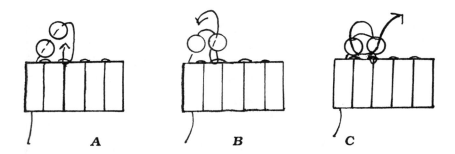

A   B   C

FRINGE

Beautiful free-swinging fringe is one of the most popular and distinguishing characteristics of beaded earrings. Within the fringe there is a lot of room for creativity and a wide variety of accent beads or other materials can be used. The bottom of the fringe is also a good place to use beads with odd sizes or shapes which can not be used elsewhere.

Fringe is added after the body (base and top) of the earring is completed. In this example the base row is comprised of bugle beads, but the procedure remains the same when seed beads are used in the base row.

Turn the earring so that the base row bead(s) with the needle and thread coming out of it is on the left. String the beads for the first fringe strand, following the order shown in whatever earring pattern is being used. Add the bottom fringe beads (which are used to anchor this end of the strand), then go back up through the rest of the beads in the fringe strand. Continue back up through the first base row bead (Figure 5A). Adjust the tension in the fringe strand; it should be tight enough so that no thread shows, but loose enough for the fringe strand to swing freely.

Figure 5 (Part I)

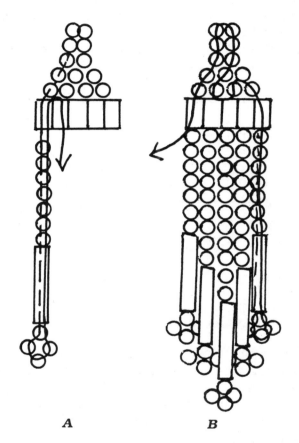

A   B

Go down through the second base row bead and add the second fringe strand in the same manner as the first. Adjust the tension in the second fringe strand and readjust the first strand if needed. Continue in this way until all the fringe strands have been added. Weave the thread through several beads in the top of the earring, then come back down through a base row bead. Cut the thread below the base row (Figure 5B).

If the earring has a large number of base beads or if the fringe is particularly long or heavy, the strands may be anchored to the body by coming up through the base row and then through one or more beads in the top before going down through the next base row bead.

A wide variety of bottom fringe designs may be used to

secure the bottoms of the fringe strands. Several possibilities
are shown in Figures 5C to 5K.

Figure 5 (Part II)

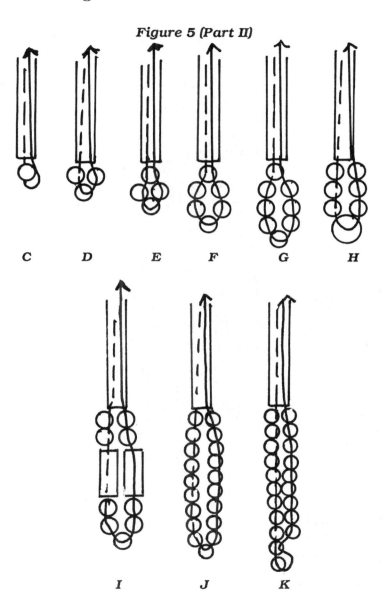

PATTERN 1: BUGLE BEAD BASE

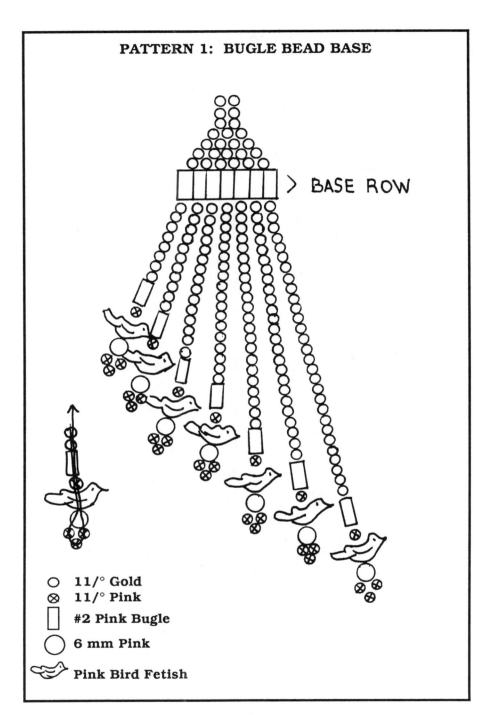

BASE ROW

○ 11/° Gold
⊗ 11/° Pink
▯ #2 Pink Bugle
◯ 6 mm Pink
🕊 Pink Bird Fetish

12

PATTERN 2: BUGLE BEAD BASE

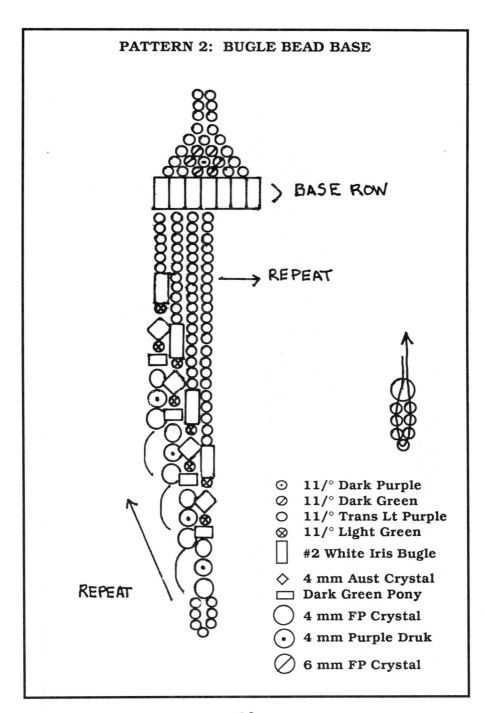

> BASE ROW

→ REPEAT

REPEAT

⊙ 11/° Dark Purple
⊘ 11/° Dark Green
◯ 11/° Trans Lt Purple
⊗ 11/° Light Green
▯ #2 White Iris Bugle
◇ 4 mm Aust Crystal
▭ Dark Green Pony
◯ 4 mm FP Crystal
⦿ 4 mm Purple Druk
⊘ 6 mm FP Crystal

13

PATTERN 3: BUGLE BEAD BASE

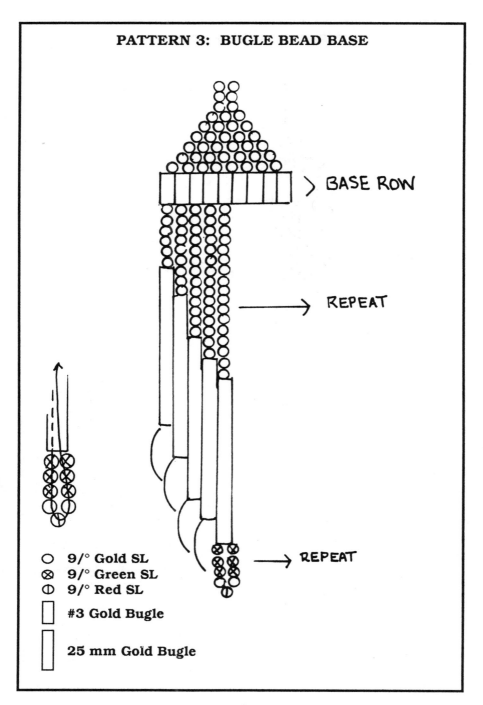

BASE ROW

REPEAT

REPEAT

○ 9/° Gold SL
⊗ 9/° Green SL
⊕ 9/° Red SL
▢ #3 Gold Bugle

▢ 25 mm Gold Bugle

14

PATTERN 4: BUGLE BEAD BASE

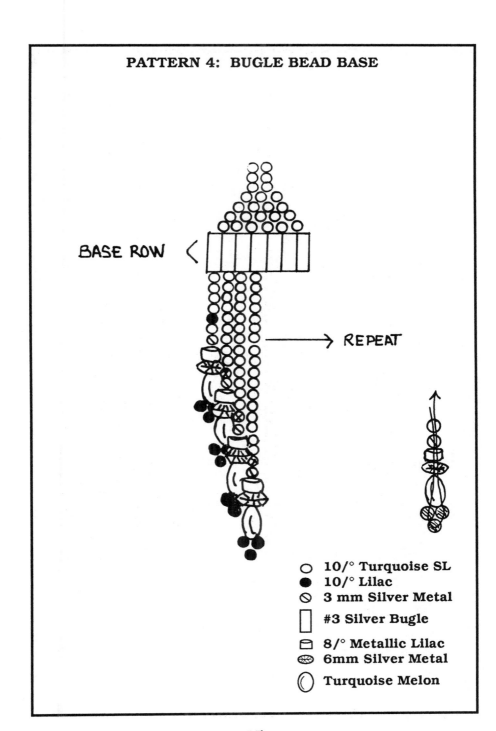

BASE ROW

→ REPEAT

○ 10/° Turquoise SL
● 10/° Lilac
⊘ 3 mm Silver Metal
▯ #3 Silver Bugle
▱ 8/° Metallic Lilac
⊛ 6mm Silver Metal
◯ Turquoise Melon

15

Page 30

Page 33

Page 50

16

COMANCHE WEAVE VARIATIONS

BUGLE BEAD TOPS

Bugle beads can be used in place of seed beads in the top of the earring. Using all bugle beads provides a different look and many new design opportunities.

To make this earring style, first complete a bugle bead base row (see Bugle Bead Base Rows). Turn the base row so that the needle and thread are on the left, coming out of the top of the first base row bead. Put two new bugle beads on the thread. Go under the thread between the second and third base row beads, from back to front. Go up through the second new bugle bead (Figure 6A). Then come down through the first new bugle bead and back up through the second new bugle bead again (Figure 6B).

Place a third new bugle bead on the thread. Go under the thread between the third and fourth base row beads, then back up through the new bugle bead (Figure 6C). Add a fourth new bugle bead and go under the thread between the fourth and fifth base row beads. Come back up through the new bugle bead (Figure 6D). If a longer base row was used, continue adding single bugle beads in the same manner until the end of the row (one less bead than in the base row) is completed.

Figure 6 (Part I)

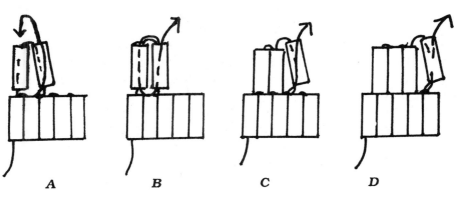

A   B   C   D

17

Turn the earring over to begin the second top row. This places the thread tail on the bottom right of the earring. Start this row with two new bugle beads and go under the thread between the second and third bugle beads in the previous row. Go back up through the second new bugle bead (Figure 6E), down through the first new bugle bead and back up through the second bugle again (Figure 6F). Add the rest of the beads in this row singly (Figure 6G). Continue adding new rows (always weaving from left to right) until a three bead row is completed.

Figure 6 (Part II)

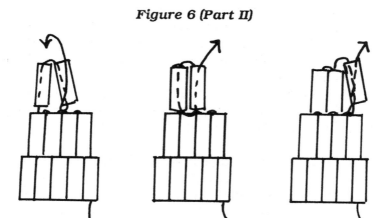

E   F   G

Put both bugle beads for the two bead row on the thread at the same time. Attach them using the same technique used at the beginning of all the other rows (Figures 6H & 6I).

Add four seed beads to form the top loop. Go down through the first two bugle beads on the left side of the earring. Come back up through the middle bead of the three bead row and through the top bugle bead on the left once again. Continue back through the four seed beads of the loop then down through the bugle beads on the right side of the earring. End by coming out through the bottom of the base bugle bead which is farthest to the right (Figure 6J). Turn the earring over so that the needle and thread are on the left. This puts the earring in the correct position to add fringe, which is the next step (see Fringe).

Figure 6 (Part III)

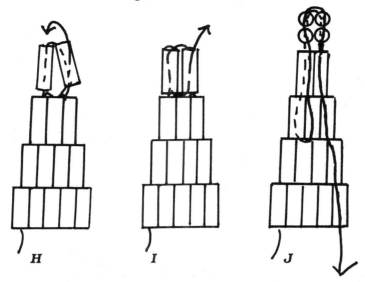

H   I   J

BUGLE AND SEED BEAD COMBINATIONS

Another way to vary the Comanche Weave is to mix seed and bugle beads in the base or top rows. The trick to using this variation effectively is to use groups of seed beads which match exactly the height of the bugle beads being used. Size 11/° seed beads may be used with #2 and #5 bugle beads, but the individual beads must still be chosen carefully. Any combination of bugle beads with seed bead sets may be used in either the base or the top rows; the sequence used here is only an example.

To begin, add one bugle bead and three seed beads to the thread (Figure 7A). Make sure that the three seed beads fit smoothly and evenly next to the bugle bead and that together they measure exactly the same height as the bugle bead (Figure 7B). Go up through the bugle bead (Figure 7C), then back down through the three seed beads (Figure 7D).

Add three more seed beads to the thread (Figure 7E). Again, these three beads must equal exactly the height of the bugle bead. Go down through the first set of seed beads (Figures 7F & 7G) and come back up through the second set of seed beads (Figure 7H).

Put another set of three seed beads on the thread and add

19

them as if they were a single bead in the base row (Figures 7I, 7J & 7K).

Figure 7 (Part I)

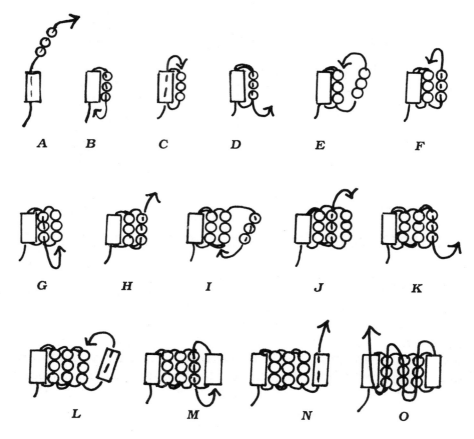

Add a single bugle bead to the end of the base row (Figures 7L, 7M & 7N). Weave back through the base row (down through the third set of seed beads, up through the second set, etc.), ending with the thread coming up out of the first base row bead (Figure 7O). The top of the earring can now be added.

Begin the first top row by adding one bugle bead and three seed beads to the thread. Remember to make sure that the seed beads fit smoothly and evenly against the bugle bead and that, as a group, they are the same height as the bugle bead. Go under the threads between the second and third bead sets in the base row. (From here on, a set of three seed beads occupying a single position in a previous row will be termed a "bead"). Come back up through the three seed beads (Figure 7P). Go down through the bugle bead and up through the three seed beads once again (Figure 7Q).

Add three more seed beads to the thread. Go under the threads between the third and fourth beads in the base row, then back up through the three new seed beads (Figure 7R).

Put a bugle bead on the thread. Go under the threads between the fourth and fifth beads in the base row and come back up through the bugle bead. (Figure 7S).

Figure 7 (Part II)

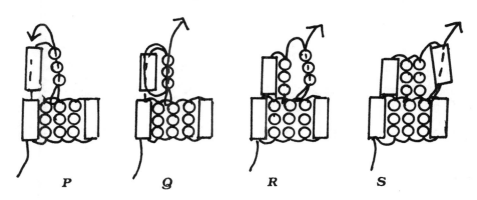

P   Q   R   S

Turn the earring over (so that the loose thread end is on the right) to begin the second top row. Add one bugle bead and three seed beads to the thread. Attach them in the same manner as the first two beads in the previous row (see Figures 7P & 7Q).

To complete this row, add a final bugle bead using the procedure already described for beads not at the beginning of a row (Figure 7T). Turn the earring over so that the loose thread is on the left.

The fourth and final row in this example consists of two bugle beads. String both of them on the thread and use the technique described for the beginning of previous rows to attach them to the rest of the earring (Figures 7U & 7V).

Add four seed beads to form the loop for attaching the ear wire. Go down through the first two bugle beads on the left edge of the earring. Come back up through the middle set of seed beads in the three bead row and continue up through the left edge bugle bead in the top row. Go back through the four seed beads of the loop and come down through all of the bugle beads on the right edge of the earring (Figure 7W). Turn the earring over so that the needle and thread are on the left and add the fringe.

Figure 7 (Part III)

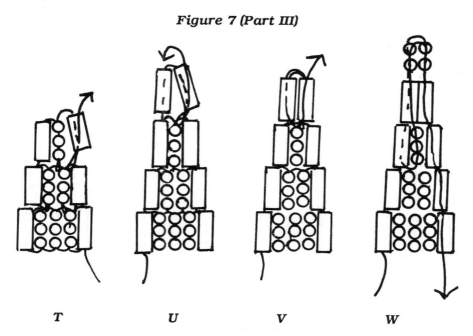

T   U   V   W

SEED BEAD BASE ROWS

Comanche Weave base rows can also be made using sets of one, two, or three seed beads in place of bugle beads. The techniques used to make a seed bead base row are the same as the techniques used for making a bugle bead base row; however, the smaller size of the beads and the use of more than one bead at a time make this type of base row more difficult to create.

To begin a one seed bead base row, string two seed beads leaving the usual six inch tail of loose thread at the end (Figure 8A). Put the two beads side-by-side and go up through the first bead (Figures 8B & 8C). Come down through the second bead (Figure 8D) and add a third seed bead to the thread (Figure 8E).

Go down through the top of the second seed bead and up through the bottom of the third seed bead (Figures 8F & 8G).

Figure 8 (Part I)

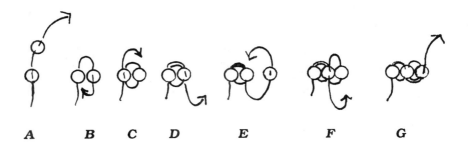

A   B   C   D   E   F   G

Add a fourth seed bead and go up through the third seed bead and down through the new (fourth) bead (Figures 8H, 8I & 8J). Continue in this manner until all of the beads have been added to the base row. Weave back through the beads in the row, ending with the thread coming out the top of the first seed bead in the row (Figure 8K).

Figure 8 (Part II)

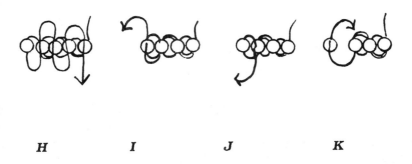

H   I   J   K

To make a two seed bead base row, use the same procedure - simply substitute two seed beads each time a single bead is called for in the instructions (Figures 8L to 8P). Make

23

sure that all the beads are the same size so that the row will have a uniform appearance.

Figure 8 (Part III)

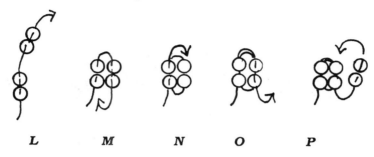

L   M   N   O   P

The same is true for a three seed bead base row (Figures 8Q to 8U).

Figure 8 (Part IV)

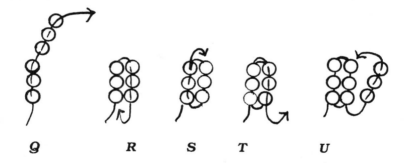

Q   R   S   T   U

TUBE EARRINGS

A simple three-dimensional variation of the Comanche Weave is the tube earring. These can be made from any Comanche Weave pattern, although some patterns look better in this form than others. The tube patterns provided in this book have wide bugle bead base rows and long fringe. The example in these instructions has a bugle bead base row and a regular seed bead top.

Make the entire earring (base, top and fringe) in the

regular manner (see instructions for the earring style chosen), but when the fringe is completed do not weave the thread up into the top of the earring and do not cut the thread.

Fold the base row of the earring into a tube with the two end beads touching (side by side). The needle and thread should be coming out of the top of one of these two beads. Take the thread down through the other bead and back up through the first bead (Figure 9A). This step can be repeated for added strength. For even more strength, go through one or two of the top beads before going through the base row beads a second time. Secure the thread ends, weaving them up into the top of the earring, then back down through one of the base row beads; then cut off any remaining thread.

Figure 9

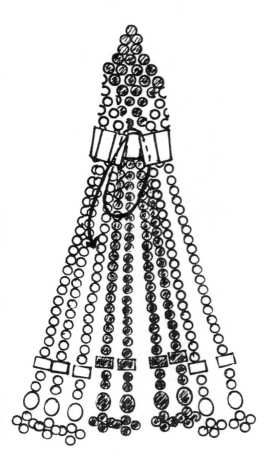

A

PATTERN 5: BUGLE BEAD TOP

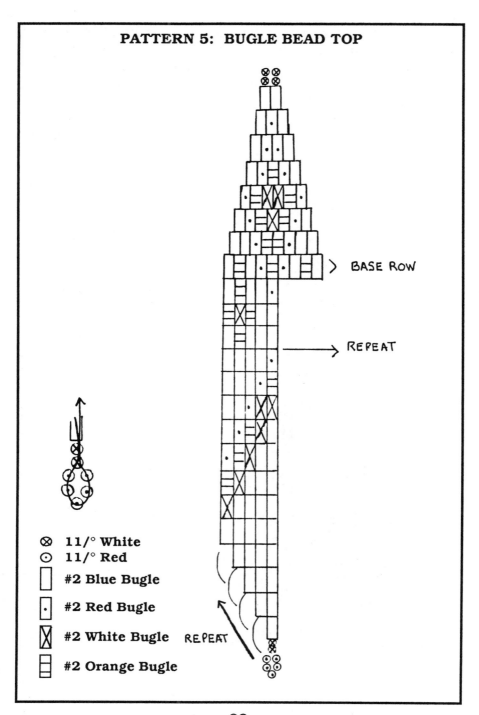

BASE ROW

REPEAT

REPEAT

⊗ 11/° White
⊙ 11/° Red
▯ #2 Blue Bugle
▯ #2 Red Bugle
▨ #2 White Bugle
▯ #2 Orange Bugle

PATTERN 6: BUGLE BEAD TOP

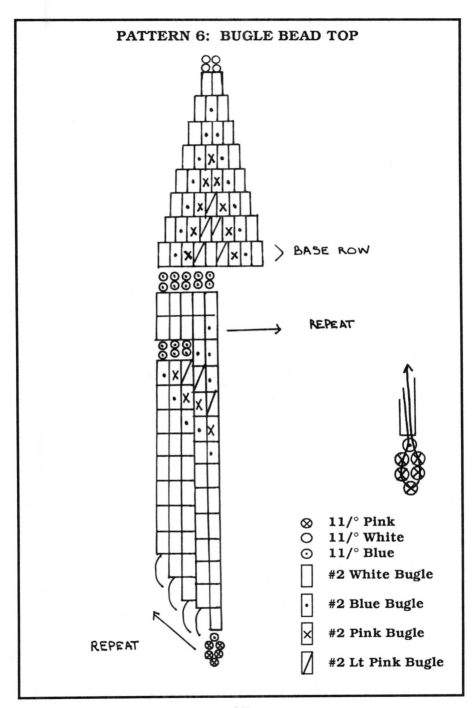

> BASE ROW

→ REPEAT

REPEAT

⊗   11/° Pink
○   11/° White
⊙   11/° Blue
▯   #2 White Bugle
▯· #2 Blue Bugle
⊠   #2 Pink Bugle
⊘   #2 Lt Pink Bugle

27

PATTERN 7: BUGLE BEAD TOP

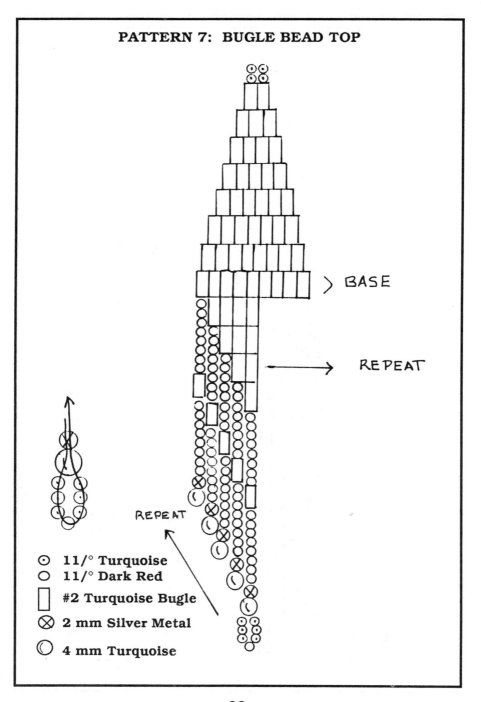

BASE

REPEAT

REPEAT

⊙ 11/° Turquoise
○ 11/° Dark Red
▯ #2 Turquoise Bugle
⊗ 2 mm Silver Metal
◖ 4 mm Turquoise

28

PATTERN 8: BUGLE BEAD TOP

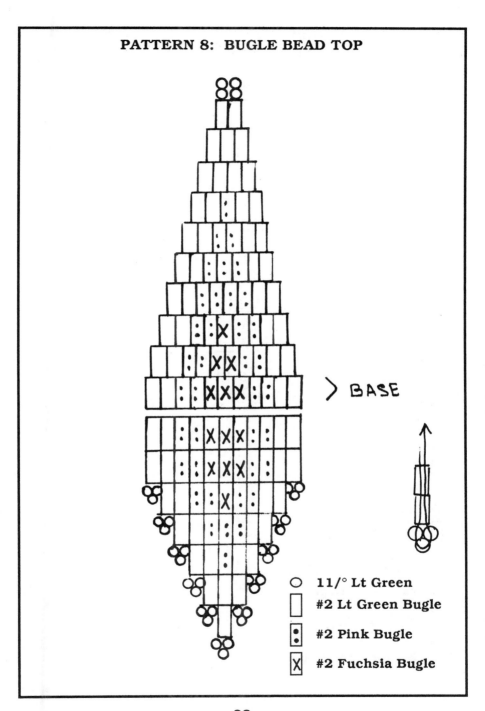

> BASE

○ 11/° Lt Green

☐ #2 Lt Green Bugle

⊡ #2 Pink Bugle

☒ #2 Fuchsia Bugle

29

PATTERN 9: BUGLE BEAD TOP

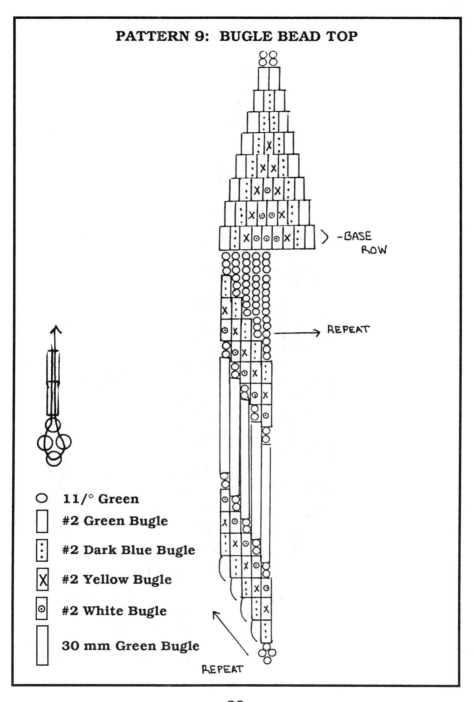

> - BASE ROW

→ REPEAT

Legend:

○ 11/° Green

☐ #2 Green Bugle

⦙ #2 Dark Blue Bugle

X #2 Yellow Bugle

⊙ #2 White Bugle

☐ 30 mm Green Bugle

REPEAT

30

PATTERN 10: BUGLE BEAD TOP

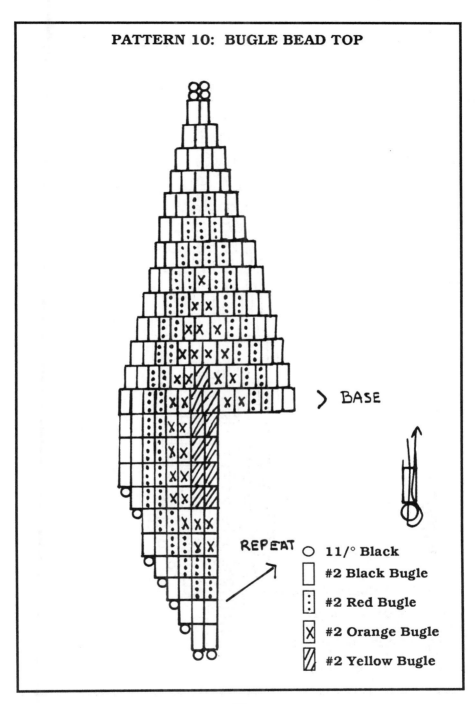

> BASE

REPEAT

○ 11/° Black

▢ #2 Black Bugle

⦙ #2 Red Bugle

☒ #2 Orange Bugle

▨ #2 Yellow Bugle

31

PATTERN 11: BUGLE/SEED COMBINATION

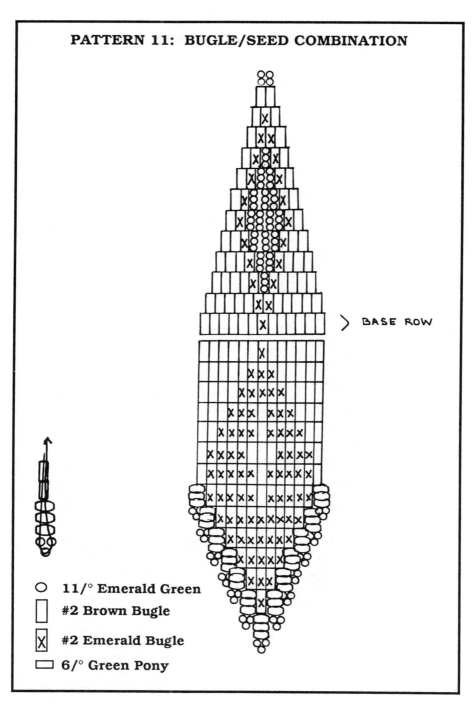

> BASE ROW

○ 11/° Emerald Green

☐ #2 Brown Bugle

☒ #2 Emerald Bugle

▭ 6/° Green Pony

32

PATTERN 12: BUGLE/SEED COMBINATION

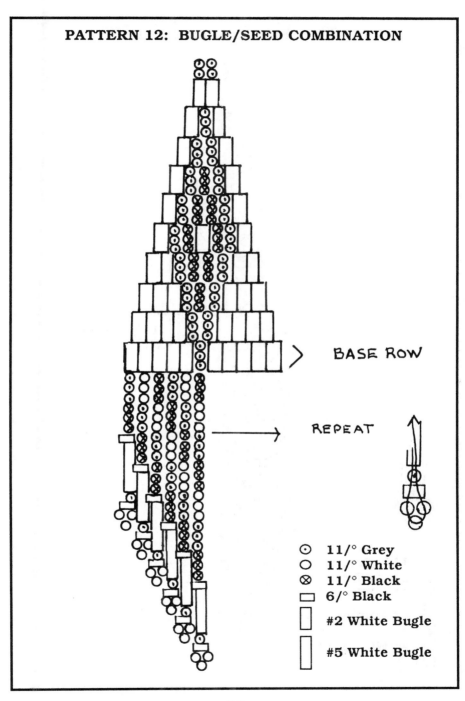

BASE ROW

REPEAT

⊙ 11/° Grey
○ 11/° White
⊗ 11/° Black
▭ 6/° Black
▯ #2 White Bugle
▯ #5 White Bugle

33

PATTERN 13: BUGLE/SEED COMBINATION

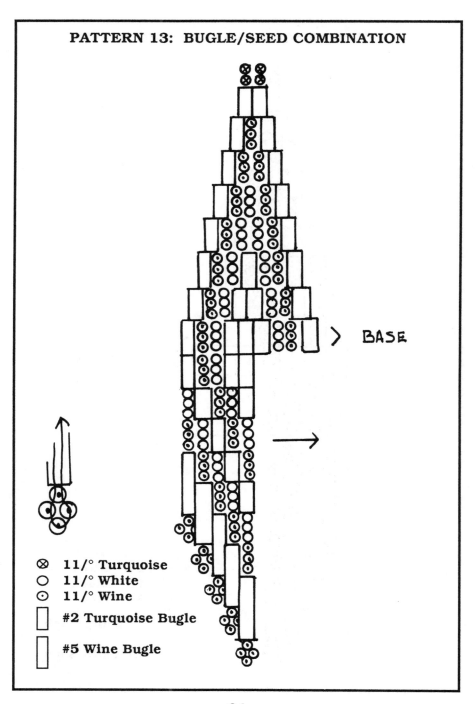

> BASE

⊗ 11/° Turquoise
○ 11/° White
⊙ 11/° Wine
▢ #2 Turquoise Bugle

▯ #5 Wine Bugle

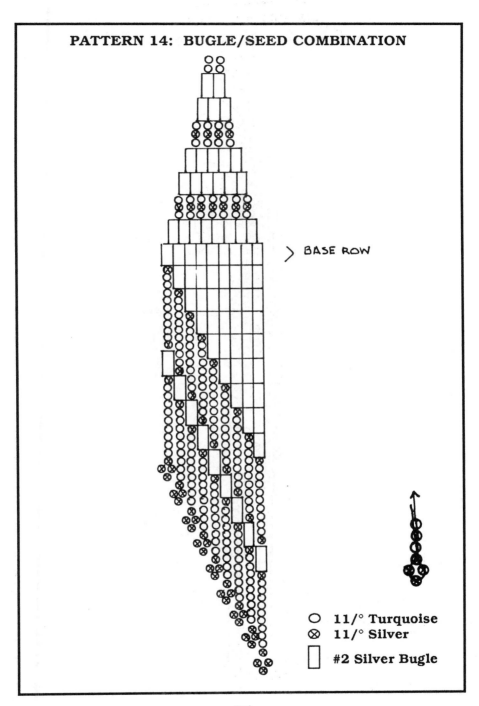

PATTERN 14: BUGLE/SEED COMBINATION

BASE ROW

○ 11/° Turquoise
⊗ 11/° Silver
▯ #2 Silver Bugle

PATTERN 15: BUGLE/SEED COMBINATION

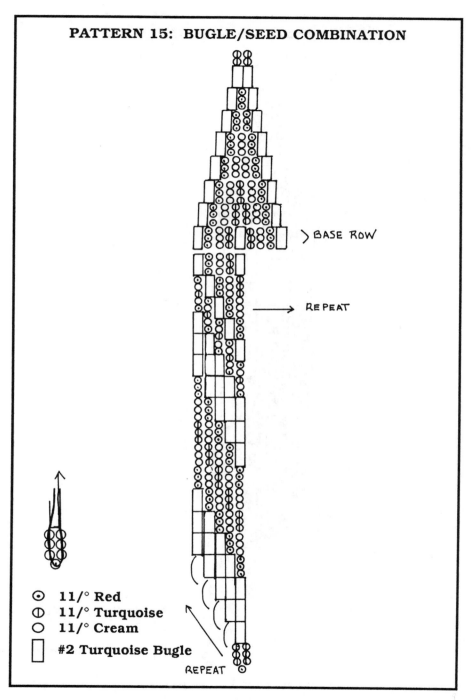

> BASE ROW

→ REPEAT

⊙ 11/° Red
⊕ 11/° Turquoise
○ 11/° Cream
▢ #2 Turquoise Bugle

REPEAT

PATTERN 16: BUGLE/SEED COMBINATION

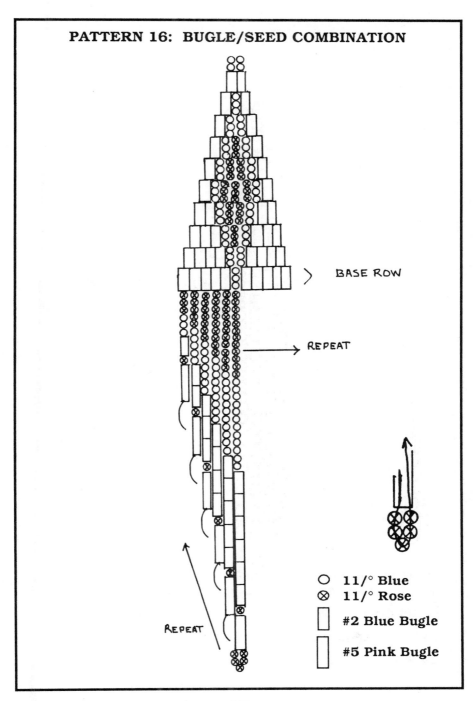

BASE ROW

REPEAT

REPEAT

○ 11/° Blue
⊗ 11/° Rose
▢ #2 Blue Bugle
▯ #5 Pink Bugle

37

PATTERN 17: BUGLE/SEED COMBINATION

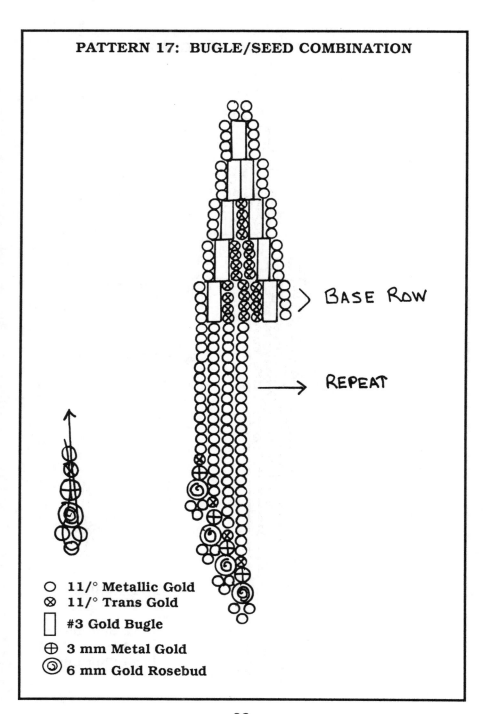

BASE ROW

REPEAT

○ 11/° Metallic Gold
⊗ 11/° Trans Gold
▯ #3 Gold Bugle
⊕ 3 mm Metal Gold
◎ 6 mm Gold Rosebud

PATTERN 18: BUGLE/SEED COMBINATION

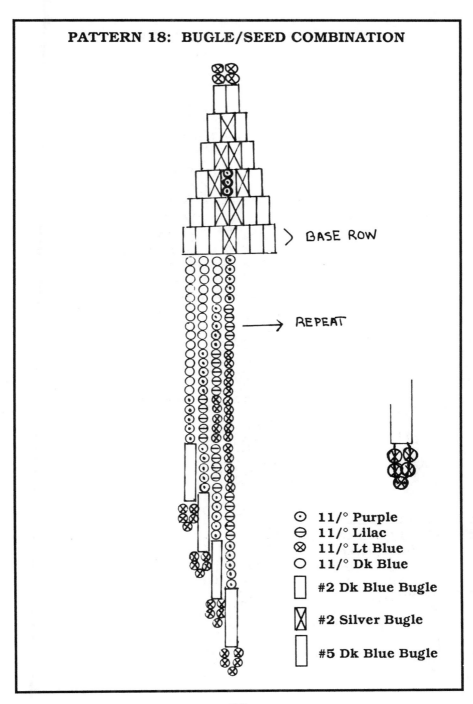

BASE ROW

REPEAT

⊙ 11/° Purple
⊖ 11/° Lilac
⊗ 11/° Lt Blue
○ 11/° Dk Blue

☐ #2 Dk Blue Bugle

☒ #2 Silver Bugle

☐ #5 Dk Blue Bugle

39

PATTERN 19: BUGLE/SEED COMBINATION

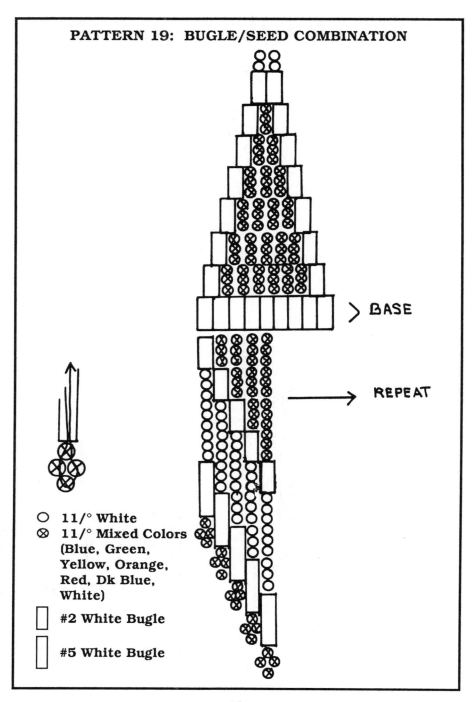

> BASE

> REPEAT

○ 11/° White
⊗ 11/° Mixed Colors
(Blue, Green,
Yellow, Orange,
Red, Dk Blue,
White)

☐ #2 White Bugle

☐ #5 White Bugle

PATTERN 20: BUGLE/SEED COMBINATION

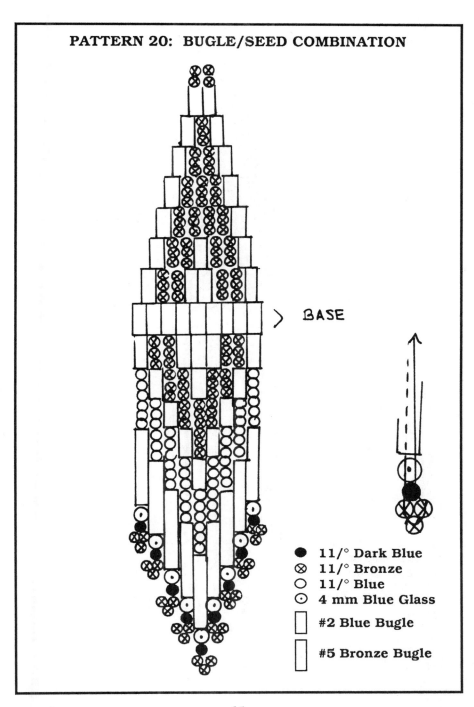

> BASE

● 11/° Dark Blue
⊗ 11/° Bronze
○ 11/° Blue
⊙ 4 mm Blue Glass
▢ #2 Blue Bugle
▯ #5 Bronze Bugle

41

PATTERN 21: BUGLE/SEED COMBINATION

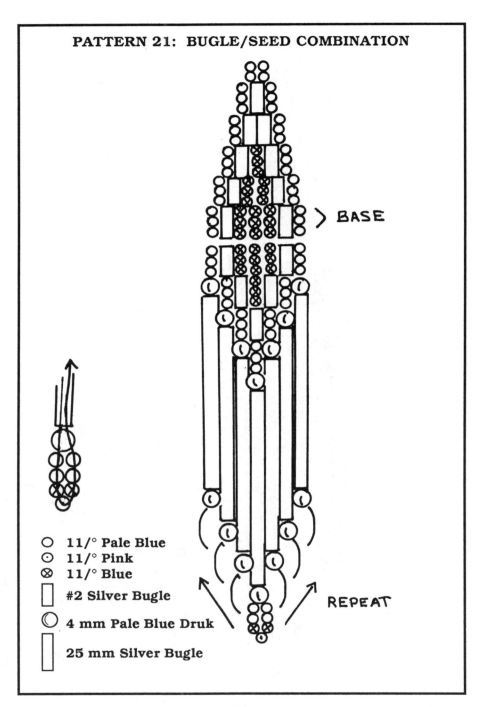

> BASE

REPEAT

○ 11/° Pale Blue
⊙ 11/° Pink
⊗ 11/° Blue
▭ #2 Silver Bugle
◖ 4 mm Pale Blue Druk
▯ 25 mm Silver Bugle

PATTERN 22: BUGLE/SEED COMBINATION

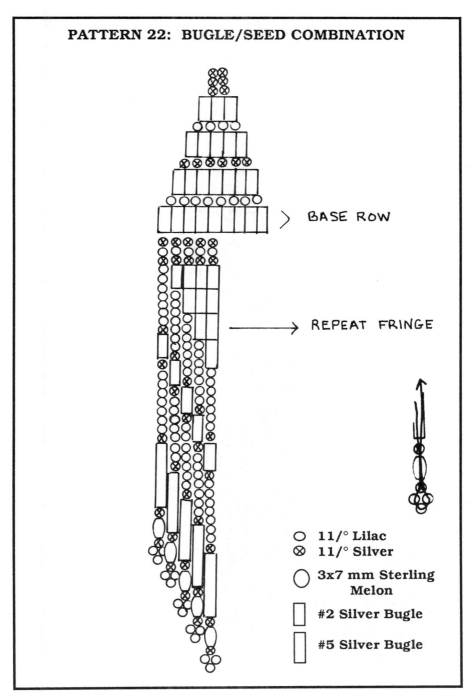

BASE ROW

REPEAT FRINGE

○ 11/° Lilac
⊗ 11/° Silver

◯ 3x7 mm Sterling
   Melon

▢ #2 Silver Bugle

▯ #5 Silver Bugle

43

PATTERN 23: BUGLE/SEED COMBINATION

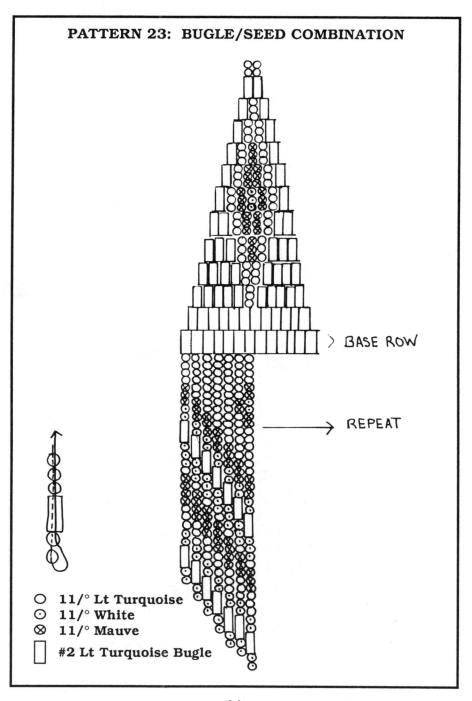

> BASE ROW

→ REPEAT

○ 11/° Lt Turquoise
⊙ 11/° White
⊗ 11/° Mauve
▢ #2 Lt Turquoise Bugle

44

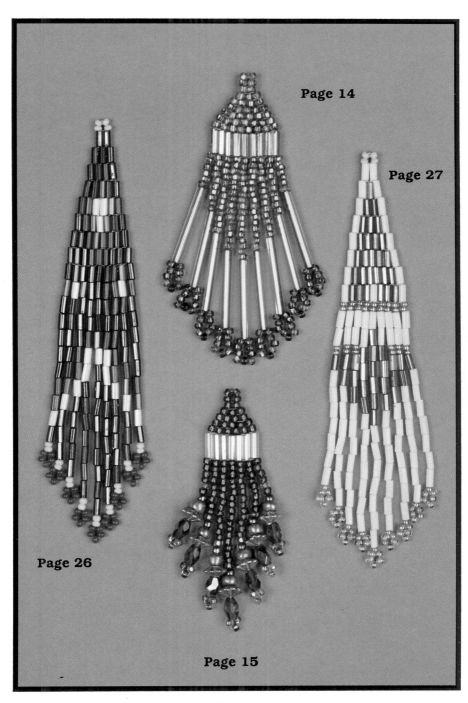

Page 14

Page 27

Page 26

Page 15

Plate I

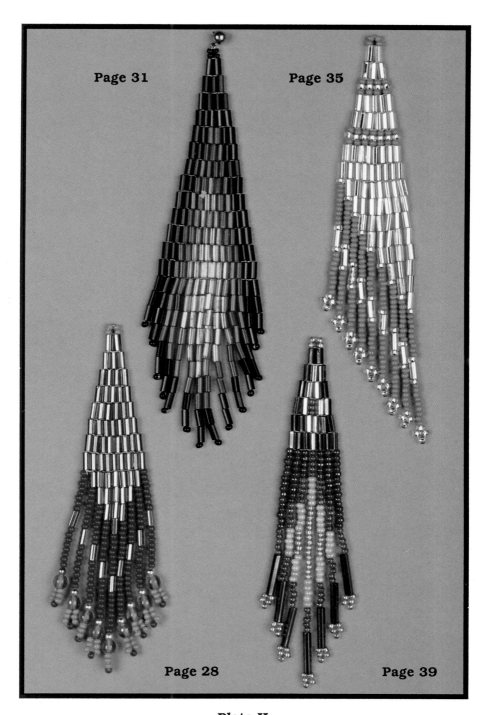

Page 31

Page 35

Page 28

Page 39

Plate II

Page 40   Page 41

Page 36   Page 42

Plate III

Page 45

Page 48

Page 43

Page 44

Plate IV

Page 49   Page 53

Page 54   Page 55

Plate V

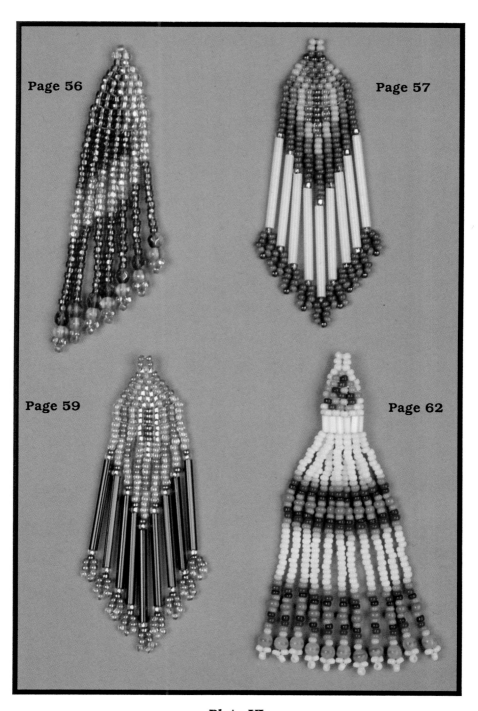

Page 56

Page 57

Page 59

Page 62

Plate VI

Page 63

Page 68

Page 69

Page 76

Plate VII

Page 77

Page 78

Page 86

Page 87

Plate VIII

PATTERN 24: BUGLE/SEED COMBINATION

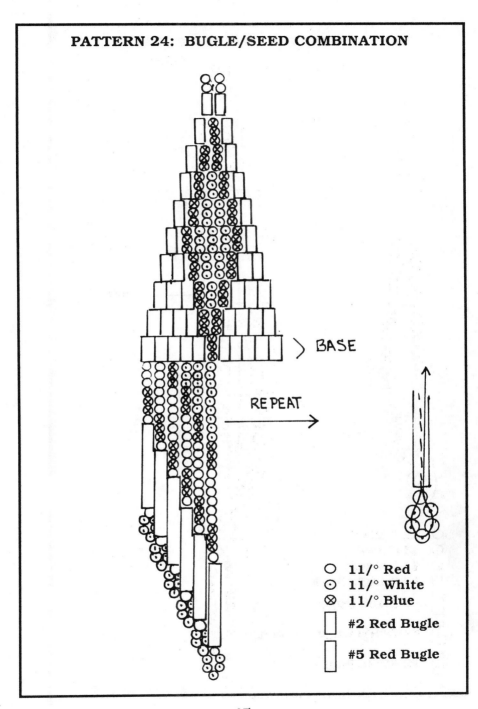

> BASE

REPEAT →

○ 11/° Red
⊙ 11/° White
⊗ 11/° Blue
☐ #2 Red Bugle
☐ #5 Red Bugle

PATTERN 25: BUGLE/SEED COMBINATION

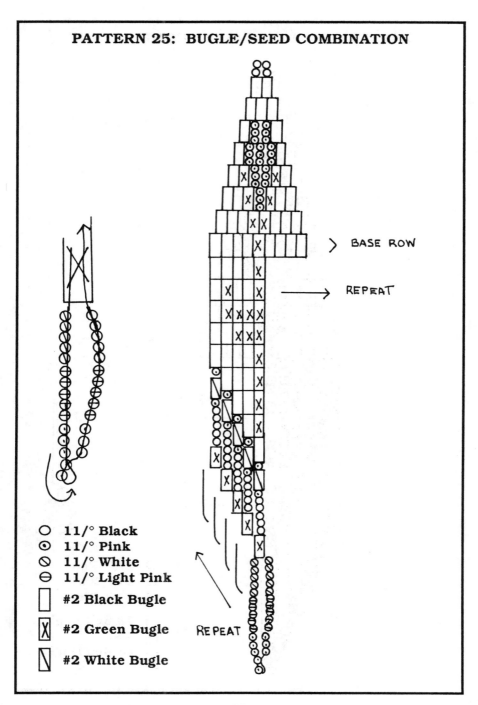

BASE ROW

REPEAT

○ 11/° Black
⊙ 11/° Pink
⊘ 11/° White
⊖ 11/° Light Pink
▯ #2 Black Bugle
☒ #2 Green Bugle
◩ #2 White Bugle

REPEAT

46

PATTERN 26: BUGLE/SEED COMBINATION

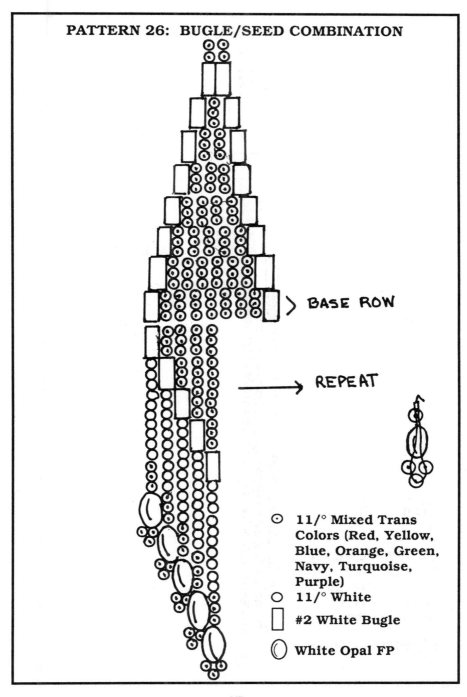

> BASE ROW

→ REPEAT

⊙ 11/° Mixed Trans Colors (Red, Yellow, Blue, Orange, Green, Navy, Turquoise, Purple)

○ 11/° White

▢ #2 White Bugle

◯ White Opal FP

PATTERN 27: BUGLE/SEED COMBINATION

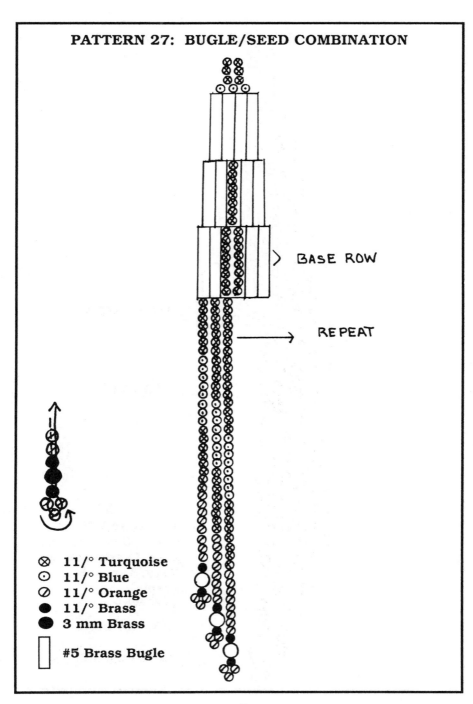

BASE ROW

REPEAT

⊗ 11/° Turquoise
⊙ 11/° Blue
⊘ 11/° Orange
● 11/° Brass
● 3 mm Brass

☐ #5 Brass Bugle

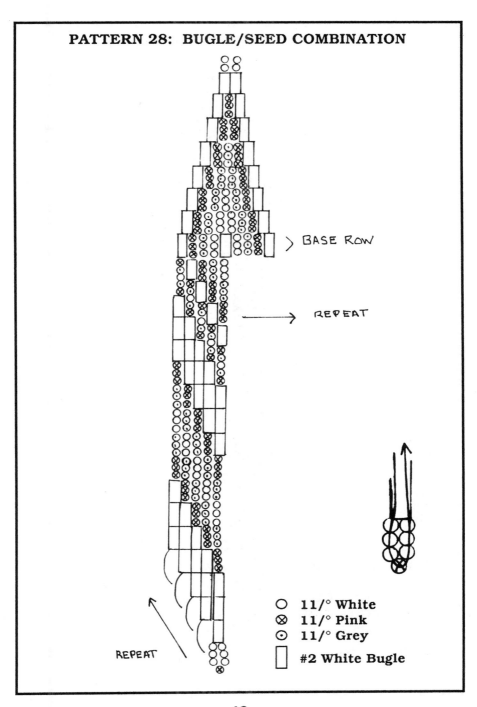

PATTERN 28: BUGLE/SEED COMBINATION

> BASE ROW

→ REPEAT

REPEAT

O	11/° White
⊗	11/° Pink
⊙	11/° Grey
☐	#2 White Bugle

PATTERN 29: DOUBLE SEED BEAD TOP

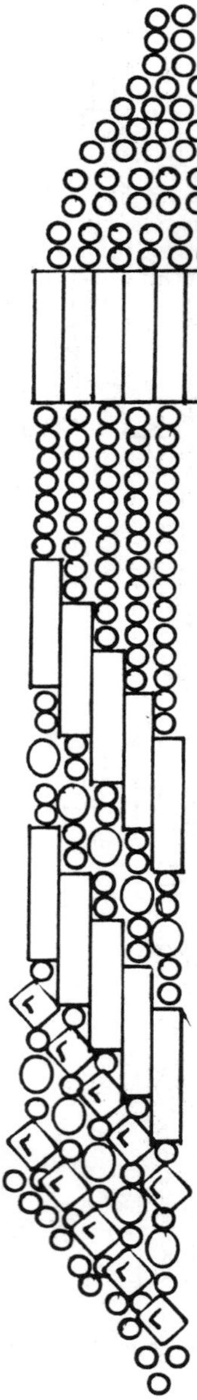

○ 11/° White/lined
   Black
◯ 4 mm Grey Glass
◇ 4 mm Grey Aust
   Crystal
▯ #5 Grey Bugle

PATTERN 30: SEED BEAD BASE

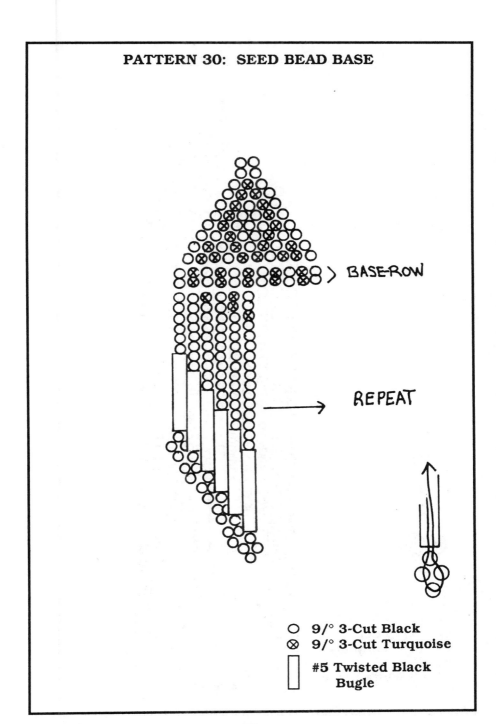

> BASE-ROW

→ REPEAT

○ 9/° 3-Cut Black
⊗ 9/° 3-Cut Turquoise
▯ #5 Twisted Black
   Bugle

51

PATTERN 31: SEED BEAD BASE

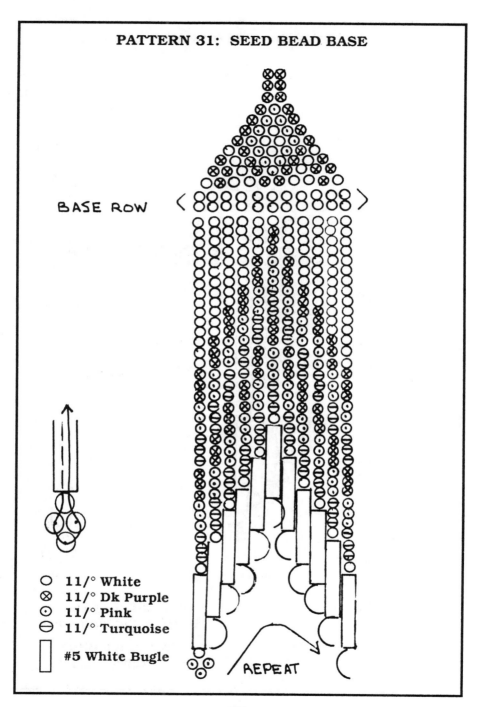

BASE ROW

○ 11/° White
⊗ 11/° Dk Purple
⊙ 11/° Pink
⊖ 11/° Turquoise

☐ #5 White Bugle

REPEAT

52

PATTERN 32: SEED BEAD BASE

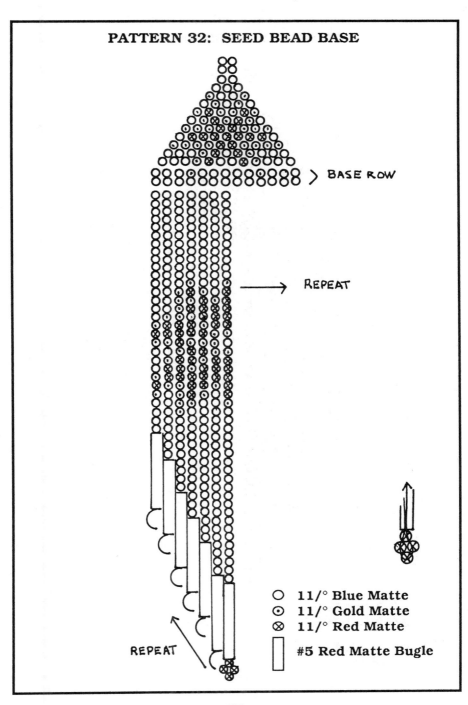

> BASE ROW

→ REPEAT

REPEAT

○ 11/° Blue Matte
⊙ 11/° Gold Matte
⊗ 11/° Red Matte

▭ #5 Red Matte Bugle

PATTERN 33: SEED BEAD BASE

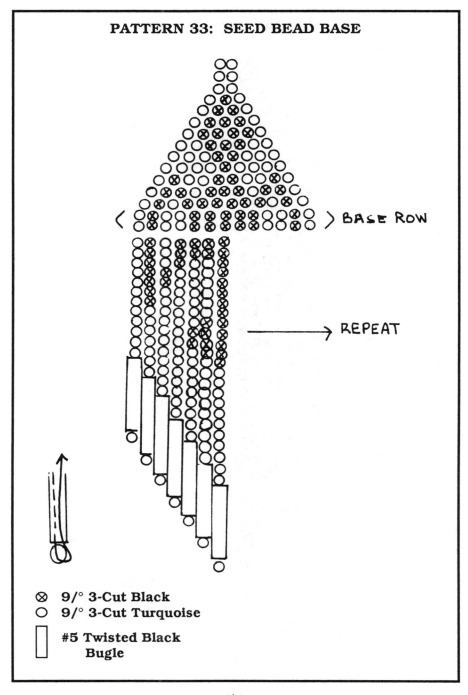

> BASE ROW

→ REPEAT

⊗ 9/° 3-Cut Black
○ 9/° 3-Cut Turquoise

#5 Twisted Black
Bugle

54

PATTERN 34: SEED BEAD BASE

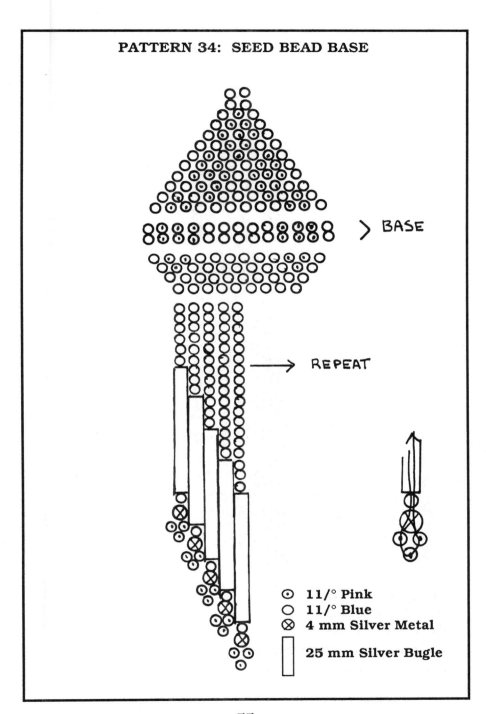

> BASE

→ REPEAT

⊙ 11/° Pink
○ 11/° Blue
⊗ 4 mm Silver Metal

▭ 25 mm Silver Bugle

PATTERN 35: SEED BEAD BASE

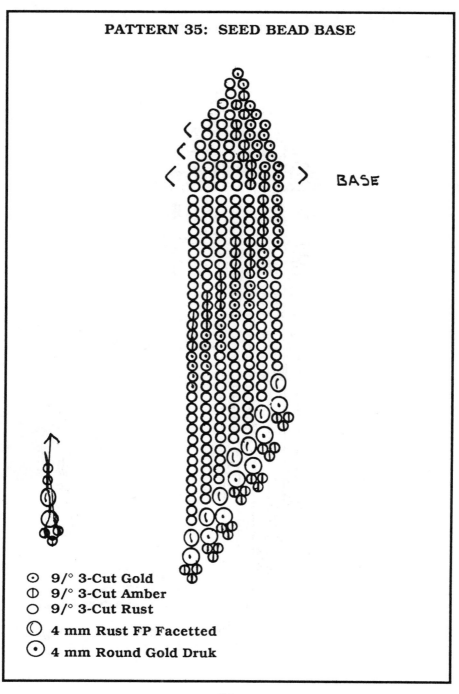

BASE

⊙ 9/° 3-Cut Gold
Φ 9/° 3-Cut Amber
○ 9/° 3-Cut Rust
◐ 4 mm Rust FP Facetted
⊙ 4 mm Round Gold Druk

56

PATTERN 36: SEED BEAD BASE

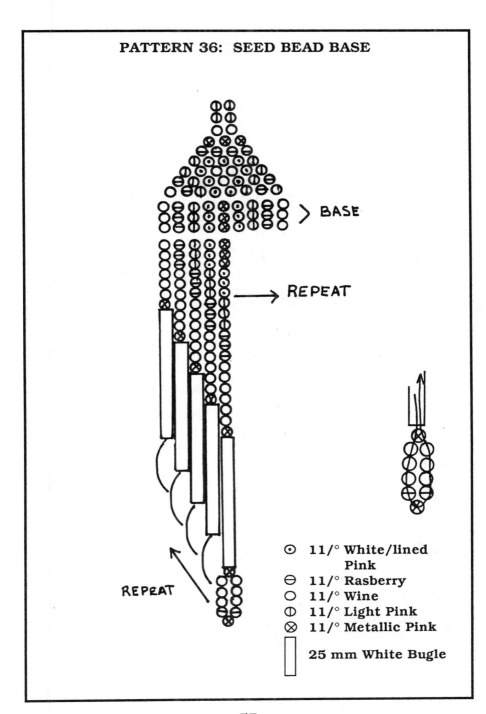

> BASE

→ REPEAT

REPEAT

⊙ 11/° White/lined Pink
⊖ 11/° Rasberry
○ 11/° Wine
⦶ 11/° Light Pink
⊗ 11/° Metallic Pink
▯ 25 mm White Bugle

57

PATTERN 37: SEED BEAD BASE

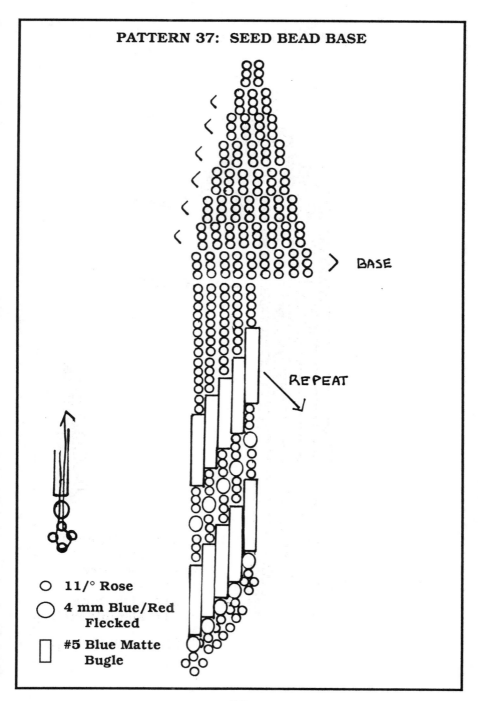

BASE

REPEAT

○ 11/° Rose

◯ 4 mm Blue/Red Flecked

▯ #5 Blue Matte Bugle

58

PATTERN 38: SEED BEAD BASE

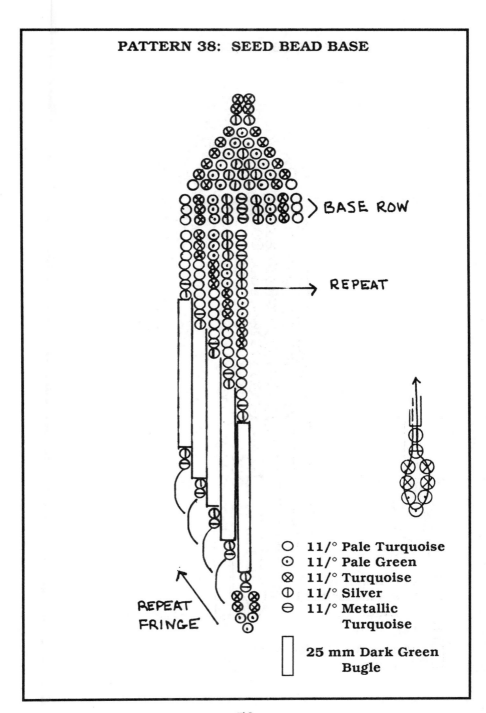

BASE ROW

REPEAT

REPEAT
FRINGE

○ 11/° Pale Turquoise
⊙ 11/° Pale Green
⊗ 11/° Turquoise
⊕ 11/° Silver
⊖ 11/° Metallic
   Turquoise

▯ 25 mm Dark Green
   Bugle

PATTERN 39: SEED BEAD BASE

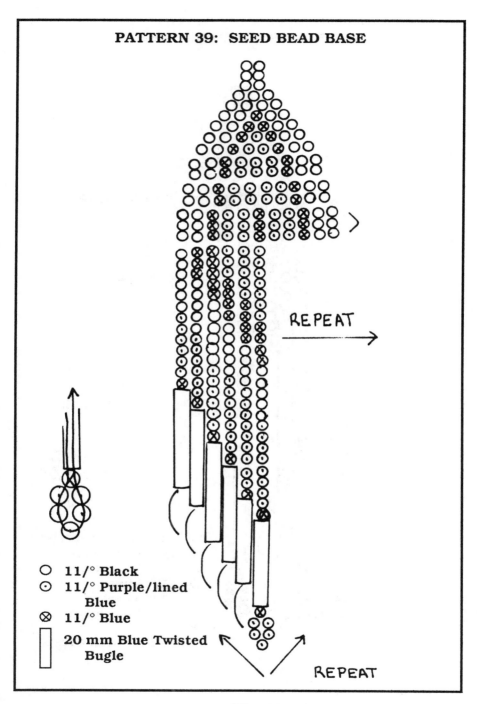

REPEAT

REPEAT

○ 11/° Black
⊙ 11/° Purple/lined
     Blue
⊗ 11/° Blue
▯ 20 mm Blue Twisted
     Bugle

60

PATTERN 40: TUBE EARRING

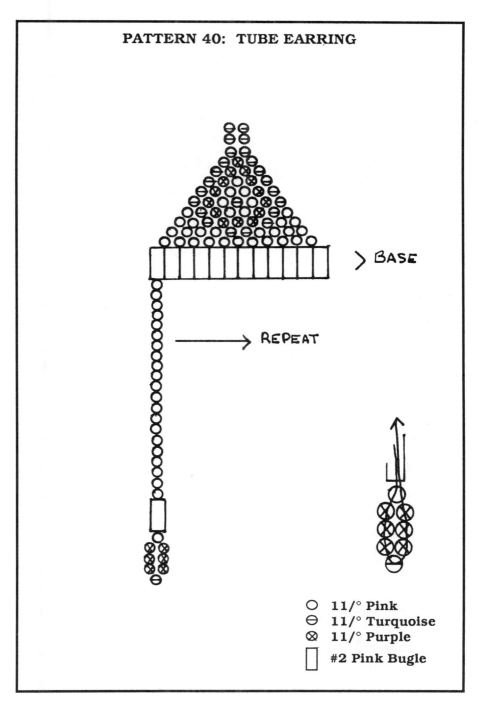

BASE

REPEAT

○ 11/° Pink
⊖ 11/° Turquoise
⊗ 11/° Purple
▯ #2 Pink Bugle

PATTERN 41: TUBE EARRING

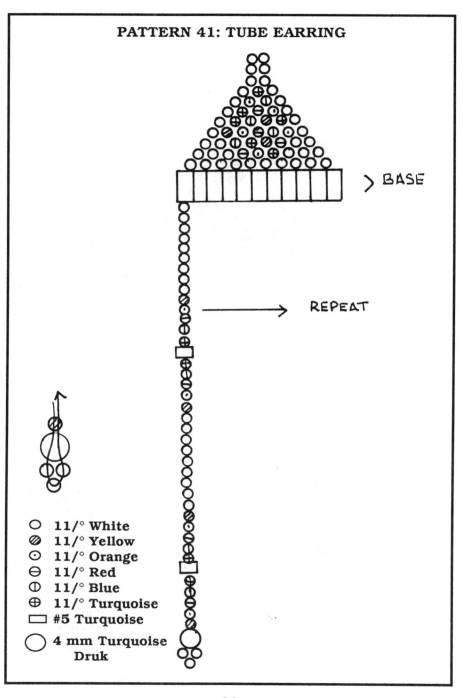

> BASE

REPEAT

○ 11/° White
⊘ 11/° Yellow
☉ 11/° Orange
⊖ 11/° Red
⊕ 11/° Blue
⊕ 11/° Turquoise
▭ #5 Turquoise

◯ 4 mm Turquoise
    Druk

PATTERN 42: TUBE EARRING

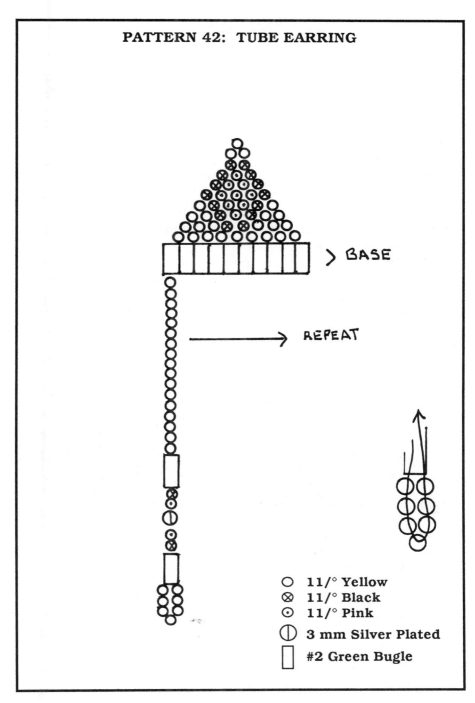

> BASE

⟶ REPEAT

○ 11/° Yellow
⊗ 11/° Black
⊙ 11/° Pink
◍ 3 mm Silver Plated
▯ #2 Green Bugle

STARS

A more complicated variation of the Comanche Weave can be used to create attractive star and half-star beaded earrings. The illustrations for the full star instructions follow Pattern 43 (with a 14 bead base row) and the illustration for the half-star instructions follows Pattern 44 (with a 16 bead base row). These instructions assume a working knowledge of the Comanche Weave technique (see Seed Bead Base Rows, Seed Bead Tops, Hiding The Thread and Fringe).

Begin this earring with the top base row indicated on the pattern. Complete the single seed bead base row according to the pattern or design desired. Place the base row at the bottom of the beadwork and bead up (it may be easiest to turn the pattern upside down for this portion of the beading). Use the Seed Bead Top technique to bead from the base row to the center row of the earring (Figure 10A).

Turn the earring over so that the base row is at the top of the beadwork. Weave the thread up through the beadwork, emerging through the fifth bead from the left end of the base row (Figure 10B).

Figure 10 (Part I)

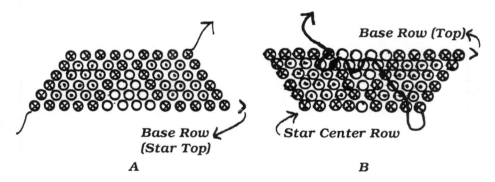

Base Row (Top)

Base Row
(Star Top)

Star Center Row

A   B

Use the two-bead technique for hiding the thread to start the top portion of the earring: string the first two beads on the thread; go under the threads between the sixth and seventh beads from the left; come up through the second bead added and go down through the first bead added. Then come back up through the second seed bead again (Figure 10C).

64

Weave the remainder of the earring top using the Seed Bead Top technique and add the earring loop (Figure 10D). Weave down to the right side of the center row to anchor the earring loop. Set this top piece of beadwork aside if a full star earring is being made.

Figure 10 (Part II)

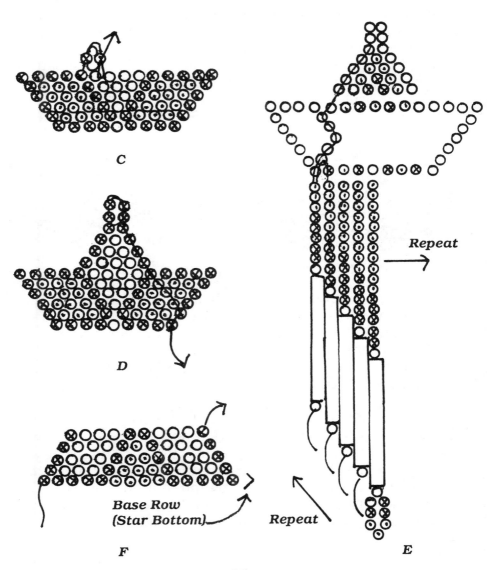

C

D

Base Row (Star Bottom)

F

Repeat

Repeat

E

65

To complete a half-star earring, flip the beadwork over so that the thread end is on the left and add the fringe according to the pattern being used (10E).

Start the bottom half of a full star with the bottom base row (see pattern). Bead up to the center of the earring using the Seed Bead Top technique (Figure 10F).

Turn the beadwork over so that the base row is at the top. As with the top half, weave the thread up through the beads, emerging through the fifth bead from the left (Figure 10G). Bead the bottom section of the earring above the base row, as was done for the top section. It may be helpful to turn the pattern upside down to bead this section (Figure 10H).

Figure 10 (Part III)

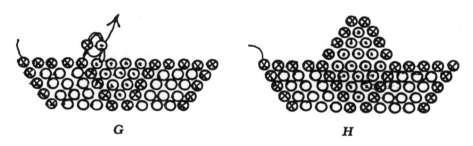

G   H

Before joining the top and bottom halves of the earring, turn the bottom piece over so that the needle and thread are at the bottom of the beadwork. Run the thread up through the right edge beads to the base row and then continue on the same diagonal up through the beadwork to the top of this piece (which will become the center of the earring). Emerge through the second bead from the right (Figure 10I).

Place the top half of the star above the bottom half, so that the two pieces can be joined. Start attaching the bottom row of the star top to the top row of the star bottom. To do this, go up through the first (right end) bead of the top half. Come down through the second bead in this row and continue down through the second (right end) bead of the star bottom again. Come up through the next (third) bead in the bottom half of the star; go back up through the second bead in the top half row, then down through the third bead in this row. Continue in this manner

66

until the last bead in the top half has been woven to the last two beads in the bottom half (Figure 10J). Weave back across to the right, reinforcing the connection between the two halves. Turn the earring over, so that the thread is on the left and weave the thread down through the bottom half of the star to the first fringe attachment point (Figure 10K). Add the fringe according to the pattern being used.

Figure 10 (Part IV)

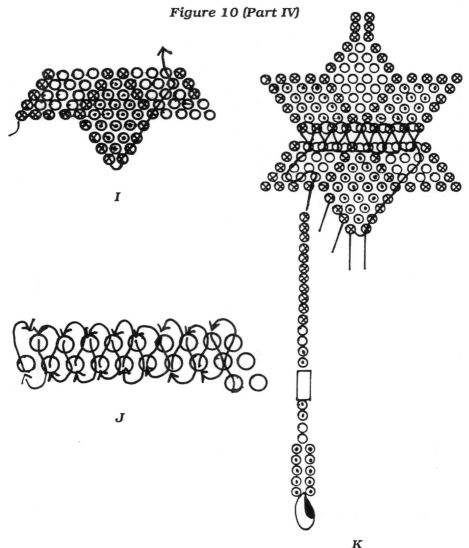

I

J

K

67

PATTERN 43: FULL STAR

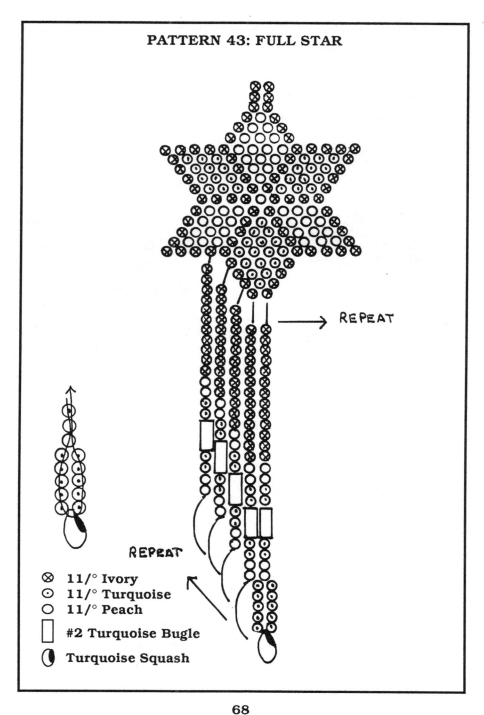

REPEAT

REPEAT

⊗   11/° Ivory
⊙   11/° Turquoise
○   11/° Peach
▢   #2 Turquoise Bugle
◖   Turquoise Squash

PATTERN 44: HALF STAR

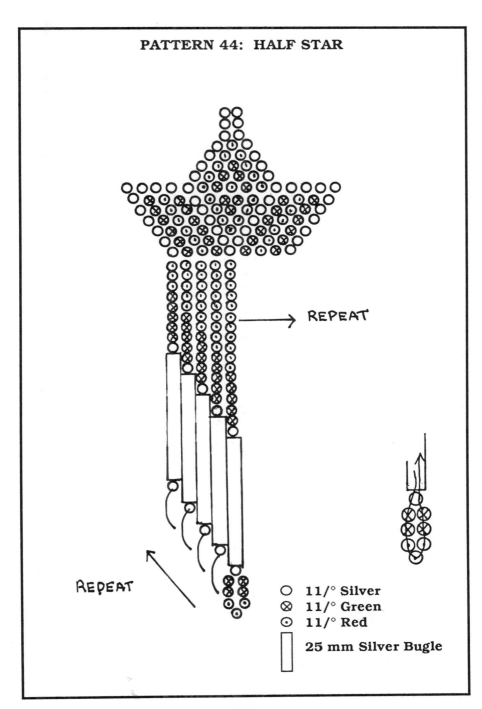

REPEAT

REPEAT

○ 11/° Silver
⊗ 11/° Green
⊙ 11/° Red

▯ 25 mm Silver Bugle

69

PATTERN 45: HALF STAR

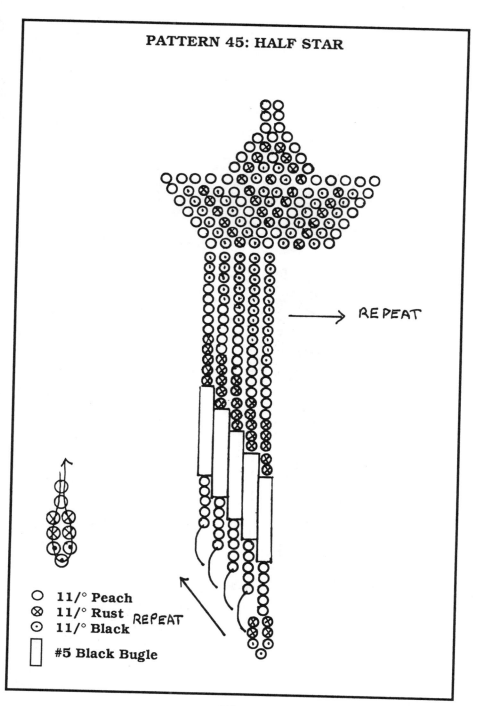

→ REPEAT

○ 11/° Peach
⊗ 11/° Rust
⊙ 11/° Black
▭ #5 Black Bugle

REPEAT

70

DIAMONDS

The diamond-shaped earrings in this book are made with either a single or two seed bead base row and with either single or two seed bead rows in the body. The illustrations follow patterns from this section. The instructions assume a working knowledge of the Comanche Weave technique (see Seed Bead Base Rows, Seed Bead Tops, Hiding The Thread and Fringe).

Begin by weaving the base row as marked in the chosen pattern; in this example a two seed-bead base is used. Follow the color design and select the size of the beads carefully to keep the row uniform (Figure 11A). Weave back through the base row to the beginning point and following the pattern, add the first top row from left to right; in this example the body rows consist of two seed beads in each position (Figure 11B).

Figure 11 (Part I)

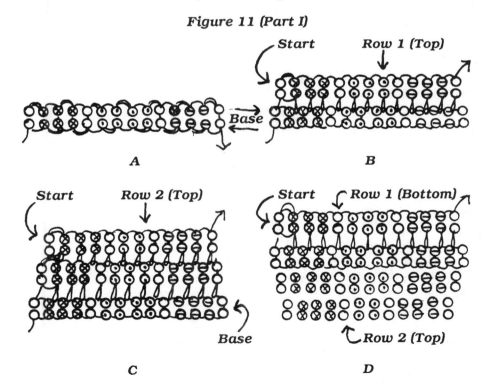

Weave back through the first top row to its starting point. Add the second top row from left to right (Figure 11C) and weave

71

back through it all the way to the left. Each row will be added in this fashion, beading from left to right, then weaving back to the left before starting the next row.

After the second top row has been added, move to the bottom of the diamond. Weave the thread down to the left edge of the base row again. Turn both the beadwork and the pattern upside down; keep the starting point of the beadwork on the left. Add the first bottom row from left to right and then weave back to the beginning of the row (Figure 11D).

Add row two (bottom) and weave back to the starting point (Figure 11E). By adding two rows above and then two rows below the base row, the earring will be more stable and will not warp when completed.

Add the remaining rows to the bottom of the diamond, using the same technique and following the pattern for color placement of the beads. When the bottom rows are completed, turn the earring and the pattern right side up. Weave up through the earring to row two of the top and finish the top rows of the diamond. Again, follow the pattern carefully.

At the top of the earring, add six beads for a top loop and attach them as for a regular seed bead top (Figure 11F). If called for in the pattern, weave down through the earring and add a single seed bead on the bottom point of the diamond (Figure 11G). If no fringe is to be added, weave through the body of the earring to secure the end of the thread and clip off any excess.

Figure 11 (Part II)

Start |Row 2 (Bottom)

Base

Row 2 (Top)

E   F   G

To add fringe, weave the thread so that it is coming out the bottom of the lowest right-hand bead in the bottom row. Ignore the single bead on the point if one has been added. Place beads of the appropriate color on the thread until the fringe length identified in the pattern has been reached (this is the length of the fringe before it is looped back up to the earring). Using Figure 11H as a guide, come up through the beads on the left side of the bottom row. Continue up through the left edge beads in the next (second) row up. Come down through the next bead set to the right in this second row and back down through the left edge beads in the bottom row.

Figure 11 (Part III)

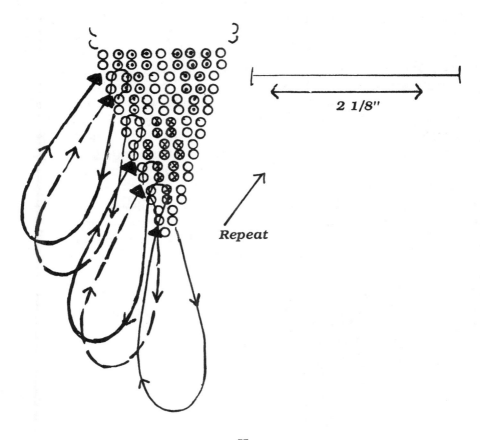

2 1/8"

Repeat

H

String the beads for the second fringe loop until the correct length is reached. Bring the needle up through the left edge beads in the third row from the bottom. Come down through the next bead set to the right in this third row and continue down through the left edge beads in the second row (see Figure 11H).

Add beads for the third fringe loop until the correct length is achieved. Go up through the left edge beads in the fourth row from the bottom. Instead of heading down, go up through the second set of beads from the left in the next row up (the fifth row from the bottom). Go down through the left edge beads in the fifth row and add the beads for the next loop (see Figure 11H).

Attach the fourth fringe loop by going up through the left edge beads of the seventh row, down through the next set of beads to the right and out through the left edge beads of the sixth row from the bottom. The beads for the fifth fringe loop are then added (if a fifth loop is called for) and this loop is attached to the first two sets of beads in the eighth row from the bottom of the diamond (see Figure 11H).

After the last fringe loop is added on the left side of the earring, weave down to the lower right-hand side of the diamond (bottom row) and repeat the same process to add the fringe on the right edge of the diamond. When all the fringe is attached, weave through the body of the earring to secure the end of the thread and clip off any excess.

The technique is the same for diamonds with single seed bead rows (Figure 11I). The length of the fringe loops need not always be the same, but can be varied (see Pattern 49).

Figure 11 (Part IV)

Fringe Length

Repeat

I

PATTERN 46: DIAMOND

> BASE

○ 11/° Silver
⊙ 11/° Green
⊖ 11/° Teal
⊗ 11/° Turquoise

75

PATTERN 47: DIAMOND

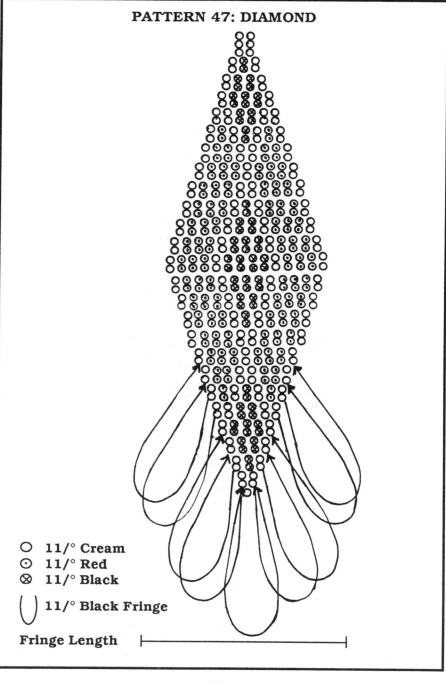

○　11/° Cream
⊙　11/° Red
⊗　11/° Black

⧙　11/° Black Fringe

Fringe Length ├─────────────────────┤

PATTERN 48: DIAMOND

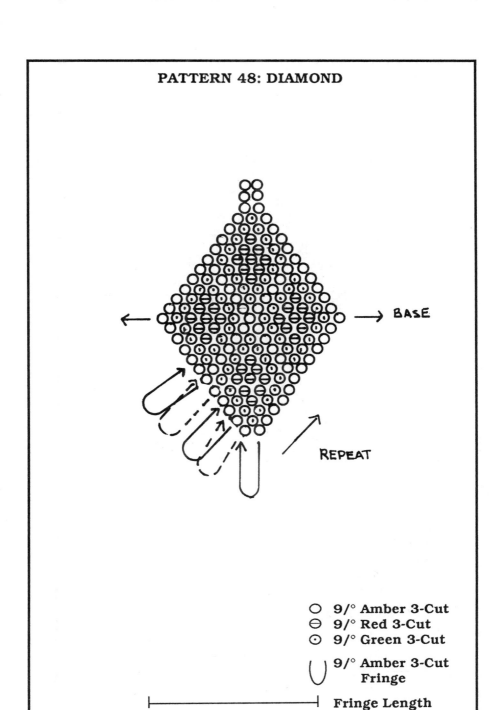

BASE

REPEAT

○ 9/° Amber 3-Cut
⊖ 9/° Red 3-Cut
⊙ 9/° Green 3-Cut

∪ 9/° Amber 3-Cut
 Fringe

├───────────┤ Fringe Length

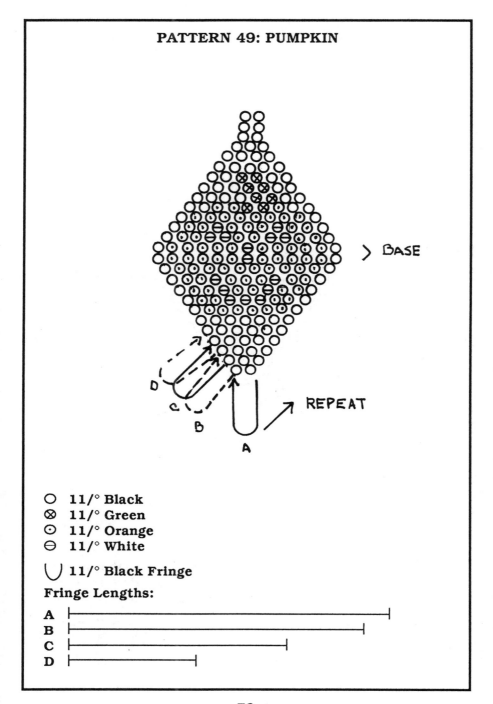

PATTERN 49: PUMPKIN

> BASE

D

C

B

A

REPEAT

O   11/° Black
⊗   11/° Green
⊙   11/° Orange
⊖   11/° White

∪   11/° Black Fringe

Fringe Lengths:

A ├───────────────────────────┤
B ├─────────────────────────┤
C ├───────────────────┤
D ├──────────┤

LACE EARRINGS

These patterns require different techniques than the Comanche Weave and can be made without any previous beading experience; however they are more complicated and thus, practice in handling beads and thread, such as can be learned with simple Comanche Weave patterns, is advisable before attempting these patterns.

Round Lace Earrings

Only one pattern is provided for this earring style, but the colors used and the color sequence of the beads may be varied. These instructions and illustrations follow Pattern 50. Bead the body of this earring in a clockwise direction.

Begin by stringing the central circle of 21 beads on the thread; follow the pattern to determine the color sequence of the beads. Go clockwise through the first three beads again to form a circle, then knot the thread to hold the circle together (Figure 12A). Take the thread through all the beads in the circle once more to reinforce this part of the earring. Emerge from one of the light pink beads in the main circle.

String three light pink beads on the thread. Skip the next two (dark pink) beads in the circle and go through the next light pink bead in the circle. String three more

Figure 12 (Part I)

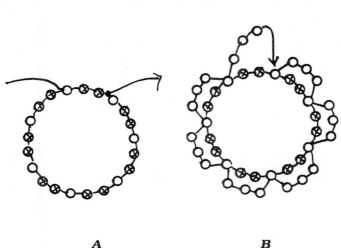

A   B

79

light pink beads, skip two dark pink beads and go through the next light pink bead in the circle. Continue in this manner, adding five more sets of three light pink beads around the circle until the starting bead is reached (Figure 12B). Weave through the sets of light pink beads again for reinforcement, emerging through the center bead of one of the three bead sets.

Add two white, one light pink and two white beads to the thread. Go through the center bead of the next three light pink bead set. String another five bead set, using the same color sequence and go through the center bead of the next three bead set. Continue around the circle, adding five more sets of five beads (Figure 12C). Weave through the five bead sets again for reinforcement and emerge through the center bead of one of the five bead sets.

Figure 12 (Part II)

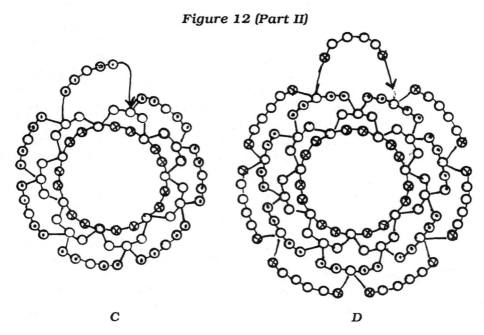

C   D

String six beads in the following sequence: one dark pink, four light pink, and one dark pink bead. Go through the center bead of the next five bead set and string on a new six bead set, using the same color sequence. Go through the center bead of the next five bead set. Add the remaining six bead sets around the outside of the earring (Figure 12D) and weave through all the

**Figure 12
(Part III)**

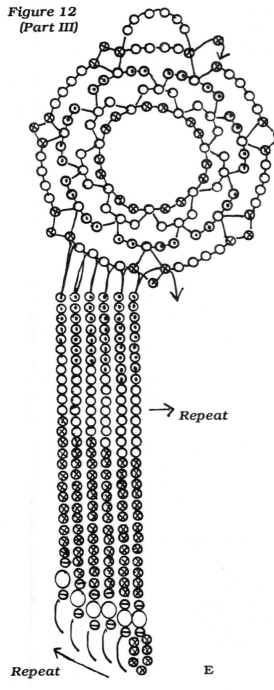

→ *Repeat*

Repeat

E

six bead sets again for reinforcement. Emerge through the last bead of one of the six bead sets.

String one dark pink bead and go through the first bead of the next six bead set. Continue through the six bead set, add one dark pink bead, then go through the next six bead set. Continue around the earring, adding single dark pink beads between each six bead set. Next add six light pink beads between the first and last beads of one of the six bead sets; this will be the top loop for attaching the ear wire (Figure 12E).

In preparation for adding the fringe, weave down through the earring to the first (left) bead of the six bead set on the bottom left of the earring. Attach the fringe segments between adjoining beads on the bottom edge of the outer

81

circle; add the fringe beads shown in the pattern, come back up through all but the bottom beads, and then go through the next bead in the six bead set on the bottom of the earring. Add the beads for the next segment and repeat the procedure just described. At the bottom center of the earring, skip the single point bead and go directly to the right six bead set (see Figure 12E). To end the earring, weave the thread back up into the center of the earring and knot the end. Clip off any excess.

It may be necessary to add more thread in the middle of beading this earring. Do this when at least eight inches of thread remain. End the old thread by weaving it to the center ring and knotting the end. Knot the end of the new piece of thread at the center of the earring and weave it through the earring to the correct position to continue beading.

Rectangular Lace Earrings

Two patterns are given for this earring style, but the colors used and the color sequence of the beads may be varied. These instructions and illustrations follow Pattern 51. Bead the body of this earring in a clockwise direction.

Start by stringing eight blue beads. Go clockwise through the first three beads to form a circle and knot the thread to hold the circle together (Figure 12F). Go through these beads twice, pushing them into a rectangular shape and reinforcing the earring. Emerge from one of the corners of the rectangle.

String three pink beads, skip one bead in the rectangle and go through the next corner bead. Continue adding sets of three pink beads between every other bead in the rectangle. Emerge through the center bead of one of the three bead sets (Figure 12G).

Figure 12 (Part IV)

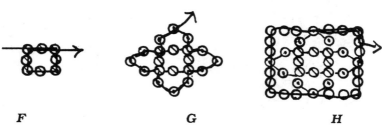

F   G   H

82

Add five white beads and go through the center bead of the next set of three pink beads. Continue adding sets of five white beads between the center beads of each three bead set until a second, outer rectangle is formed. Go through this second rectangle twice for reinforcement (Figure 12H). Emerge through the fourth bead of one of the five white bead sets.

The next sets of beads go between the fourth and second beads of adjoining five bead sets. Go through the second, third and fourth beads of each five bead set (around the rectangle corners) to end each new set and position the thread for the next set. Add sets of six blue beads to the top and bottom of the rectangle and sets of seven blue beads on each side. Reinforce these new sets (and the corners) twice (Figure 12I). Emerge from the fifth bead of one of the seven bead sets.

Put nine white beads on the thread and go through the two center beads of the six bead set on the bottom of the earring. Add another nine white beads and go through the third, fourth and fifth beads of the other seven bead set (Figure 12J). Continue up through the outside beads of the earring and reinforce the top six bead set which will be the top attachment loop.

Figure 12 (Part V)

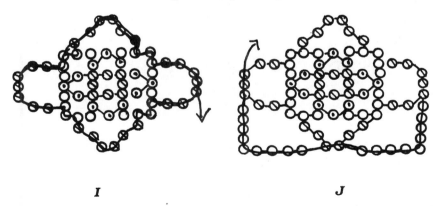

I   J

In preparation for adding the fringe, weave down through the body of the earring, emerging through the bottom of the left corner bead on the outer rectangle. Attach the fringe segments between adjoining beads on the bottom edge of the rectangle; come out of the corner bead, add the fringe segment beads, come

Figure 12 (Part VI)

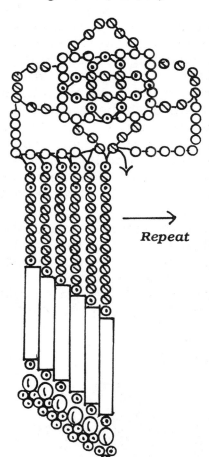

Repeat

K

back up through all but the bottom beads and continue up through the next bead in the bottom of the rectangle. Add the beads for the next fringe segment and repeat the procedure just described. Follow the color sequence in the pattern carefully (Figure 12K). To end the earring, weave the thread back up into the center of the earring and knot the end. Clip off any excess.

It may be necessary to add more thread in the middle of beading this earring. Do this when at least eight inches of thread remain. End the old thread by weaving it to the top center of the outside rectangle and knotting the end between two beads. Knot the end of the new piece of thread near the top center and weave it to the correct position to continue beading.

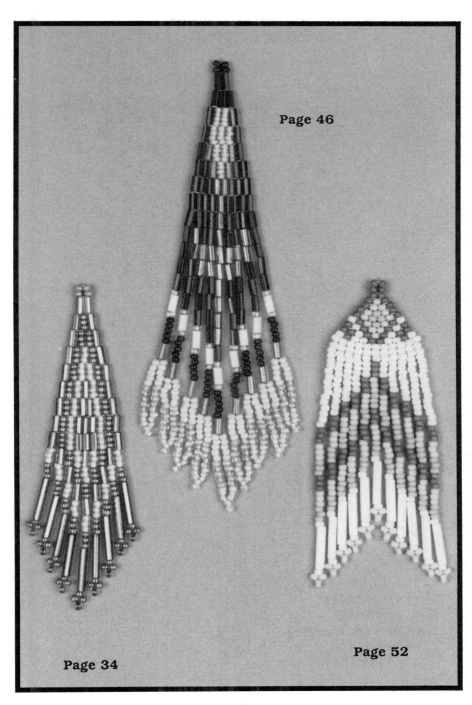

Page 46

Page 34

Page 52

85

PATTERN 50: ROUND LACE

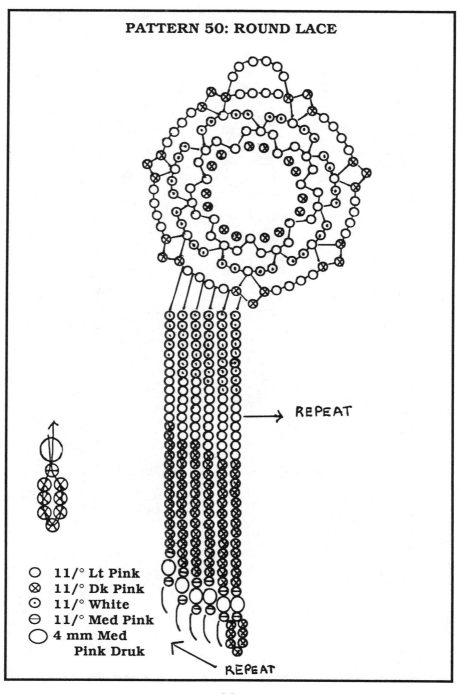

REPEAT

REPEAT

○ 11/° Lt Pink
⊗ 11/° Dk Pink
⊙ 11/° White
⊖ 11/° Med Pink
◯ 4 mm Med
    Pink Druk

PATTERN 51: RECTANGULAR LACE

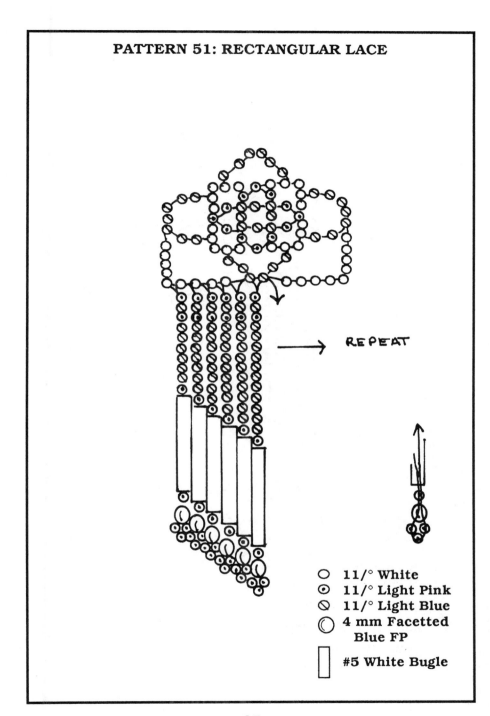

REPEAT

○ 11/° White
◉ 11/° Light Pink
⊘ 11/° Light Blue
◖ 4 mm Facetted
   Blue FP
▯ #5 White Bugle

PATTERN 52: RECTANGULAR LACE

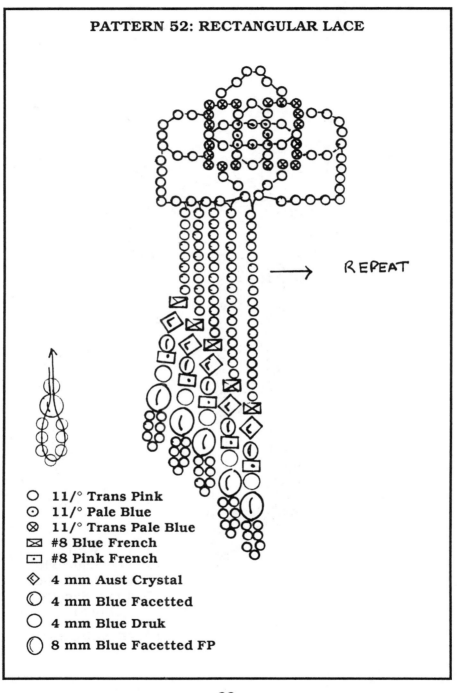

REPEAT

- ○ 11/° Trans Pink
- ⊙ 11/° Pale Blue
- ⊗ 11/° Trans Pale Blue
- ⊠ #8 Blue French
- ⊡ #8 Pink French
- ◈ 4 mm Aust Crystal
- ◖ 4 mm Blue Facetted
- ○ 4 mm Blue Druk
- ◖ 8 mm Blue Facetted FP

EARRING DESIGNS BY SIG: BOOK II

by Sigrid Wynne-Evans

Strike gold with this exciting new book from successful author and designer Sigrid Wynne-Evans. Sig has created quite a stir among beaders with her imaginative designs which feature pictures or images made from beads rather than standard geometric patterns. Both experienced and beginning jewelry makers will cherish this treasure trove of forty-six unique earring designs, all made with the Brick (or Comanche) Stitch technique. The designs will also thrill applique beadworkers who can incorporate these fresh ideas into their projects. Both contemporary and Native American themes are explored.

This book features complete, illustrated instructions, bead-by-bead patterns for each of the projects, eight pages in full color and is a must for anyone interested in creating beauty with beads.

The introduction provides basic information on beads, needles, thread, workspace and organization, as well as some thoughts on the business of selling finished beadwork. This is followed by a complete set of illustrated instructions for making Diamond and Triangle earrings with the Comanche Weave or Brick Stitch technique.

Designs included are: Apple, Shamrock, Fishes, Cockatiel, Witch, Kachina, Moo, Gemini, Guitar, Pisces, Lady Bug, Zebra, Poinsettia, Libra, Giraffe, Seagull, Buffalo Head, Forget Me Nots, Butterfly 2, Balloons, Flamenco Dancer, Unicorn, Sailboat, Girl & Moon, Raccoon, Corn, Eve, Adam, Rose, Bug, Cat Eyes, Eagle Mask, Sagittarius, Merlin, Rainbow Goddess, Sun Goddess, Koala, Shaman, Chile Pepper, Owl, Carousel Horse, Eagle, Clown, Butterfly 1, Rocking Horse and Duck with Hearts.

DELIGHTFUL BEADED EARRING DESIGNS

by Jan Radford

Welcome to a whole new world of beaded earring designs! It is hard to find a better value than this book - it is packed with a total of 81 new earring patterns and there is a black and white picture of each design right next to the pattern! Add four full color pages, featuring examples of the fourteen different earring styles, easy-to-follow, illustrated instructions and an explanation of beading supplies and this little dynamo can't miss.

New author Jan Radford teaches a variation of the Brick or Comanche Stitch which builds the foundation row and the dangles at the same time. She then explains how to expand on this technique to produce earrings with new and different looks. Her designs feature a wide range of color combinations and earrings of many different sizes. Included are geometric designs, with both contemporary and Native American themes; thunderbirds; eagles; flowers; a cross; a hound-dog face; Santa Claus and elf faces, American flags and a white, black and silver pattern called the Eye.

Earring styles include: Bugle Bead Foundations with Single-Beaded Tops, Double-Beaded Tops, and Triple-Beaded Tops; Double-Beaded Seed Bead Foundations with Single-Beaded Tops, Double-Beaded Tops, and Triple-Beaded Tops; Triple-Beaded Seed Bead Foundations with Single-Beaded Tops and Triple-Beaded Tops; Loop Dangle Earrings; Single Seed Bead Foundations; Earrings with Vertical Rows rather than horizontal ones (such as the rectangular American flags and the Eye); Triangular Post Earrings; and Earrings with Porcupine Quills or Long Bugle Beads in the dangles.